Entrepreneur

MARKET YOUR BUSINESS

Your Guide To Do-It-Yourself Marketing

JEANETTE MAW McMURTRY

Entrepreneur Press®

Entrepreneur Press, Publisher
Cover Design: Andrew Welyczko
Production and Composition: Alan Barnett Design

Library of Congress Cataloging-in-Publication Data
  Names: McMurtry, Jeanette Maw, author. | Entrepreneur Press, issuing body.
  Title: Market your business : your guide to do it yourself marketing / by
    Jeanette Maw McMurtry, MBA.
  Description: Irvine, CA : Entrepreneur Press, [2024] | Includes index. |
    Summary: "This book aims to equip you with practical insights into how
    consumers select brands, cultivate loyalty, and execute effective
    marketing strategies, even as a team of one"—Provided by publisher.
  Identifiers: LCCN 2024008269 (print) | LCCN 2024008270 (ebook) | ISBN
    9781642011661 (paperback) | ISBN 9781613084793 (epub)
  Subjects: LCSH: Marketing—Management. | Branding (Marketing)
  Classification: LCC HF5415.13 .M36943 2024 (print) | LCC HF5415.13
    (ebook) | DDC 658.8—dc23/eng/20240314
  LC record available at https://lccn.loc.gov/2024008269
  LC ebook record available at https://lccn.loc.gov/2024008270

Contents

CHAPTER 3

Understanding the Real Drivers of Choice 39

CHAPTER 4

Building Customer Experiences for Sales and Loyalty. 53

Introduction

Why Not Me? Why Not Now?

This was the mindset that propelled my three young daughters as they participated in youth sports, learning to set goals and accomplish personal bests. As a parent, the best entertainment was watching their ski races and soccer games and seeing them develop the wonderful life skills that come from competing and being part of a team. As they grew out of recreational teams to club and school teams, it didn't take long to notice which kids broke out the fastest and dominated the starting line ups. In every sport, a big contributing factor for success was DNA. Size, bone structure, and other genetic elements of physicality were common threads found in most kids getting to the top of their sport from childhood to college or even beyond. No matter an individual's hard work or mental acuity toward a sport, genetics will always be a leading differentiator in success, for youth and professionals. You can't ignore the hard fact that a 5-foot-5, 155-pound male that worked every single hour of every single day to make three pointers and never miss an easy layup simply could not do much of either against the looming physique of 6-foot-11, 284-pound Nicola Jokic, a National Championship MVP and multi-time season MVP for the Denver Nuggets; or 6-foot-9, 250 pound LeBron James. And, a height-challenged quarterback cannot suddenly see over large offensive and defensive line players to see receivers down field by working harder than anyone else does. No memes, inspirational quotes or self-help books are going to change the laws of gravity, physics, and human anatomy. And so, Virginia, some dreams simply cannot come true.

Yet in business, the playing field is much more level, and hard work has a far greater chance of paying off. In many cases, the key differentiator between those that succeed and those that do not is often marketing and adaptability. A classic example is WordPerfect and Microsoft. Back in the day, WordPerfect was reputed to be a superior product, but the founders of Microsoft executed far better marketing and branding programs. For whatever reasons, WordPerfect could or would not adapt to remain competitive. It didn't take long for the former to go out of business and for the latter to not just dominate, but own its category.

Success, if built on the right foundation, can come equally to entrepreneurs in all categories. It depends on elements equally available to all functioning humans regardless of winning DNA lotteries, which include:

> An actionable idea that is relevant for target purchasers and consumers.

> A plan for how you can most effectively manifest that idea.

> Devotion to continuously develop the knowledge and skills needed to make that plan succeed.

> Willingness to put in the time, partner with others, seek help when you need it.

> Commitment to making execution of your plan routine.

> Courage to try, fail, try again, adapt as needed, and keep moving forward toward the realization of an actually realistic goal.

> Passion about a purpose bigger than yourself and your desired wealth.

> Grit.

The catalyst to all the above driving a successful enterprise is marketing. Smart, meaningful, customer-centric, and sustainable marketing. Yet with an ever-growing abundance of marketing tools and tactics, some useful and many not, rapidly changing market dynamics, and an increasingly demanding consumer population, it's hard to know where to start, what to do, and what to expect.

The purpose of this book is to provide you with a working knowledge of how consumers choose brands and assign loyalty, and what marketing tools and tactics can be executed by a team of one and actually pay off. You'll learn how to engage consumers emotionally and psychologically, put together a plan, execute winning activities for SEO, digital and content marketing, lead generation and conversion. And you'll gain insights on what tools you need, and which you don't, and step-by-step guidance for executing a successful, affordable marketing plan.

Each chapter outlines critical concepts and key action items to get you started, setting you up to have a complete and actionable marketing plan you can execute yourself as you turn the last page. Read this book in order. Or not. But read it all and take the time to do the "Go Time" exercises at the end of each chapter. Otherwise this is just another book you failed to act upon.

As you apply the learnings in this book, keep a wide-open eye on what's happening in your markets as you build your business plan, and be ready to adapt on the fly. Change is not just constant, its rapid in our era of business, and as game-changing technology such as artificial intelligence continues to explode, so does the nature of business and consumers' expectations. Adapting to environmental, consumer, and technical change is the key to success because no amount of marketing, no matter how brilliant or broad reaching it might be, can compensate for a product or business model that is not current in the eyes of the beholder.

The bottom line…Any entrepreneur, including you, that is willing to stay the course, put in the time, and complete the daily to-do lists, will not just rise, but thrive.

So why not you? Why not now?

Let's get started.

PART 1

SETTING UP FOR SUCCESS

With the technology available today, marketing has never been so simple, or complex. Simple because you can craft personalized "mass" communications in minutes with sophisticated software tools, and complex because customers have never had so many expectations for brands with whom they choose to do business. Consumers expect you to know all about them, deliver memorable experiences, and commit to high levels of corporate social responsibility.

To succeed, you need to understand the complexities of consumers, how they make decisions and assign loyalty, and the markets in which you operate. This section will help you define the value you offer beyond the products you sell, address increasing expectations for corporate social responsibility and environmental and social governance, and tap into the psychology of choice for your customers. You'll also learn how to monitor your markets to identify risks and opportunities, and understand the psychology that drives engagement, trial, and sales.

CHAPTER 1

Define Your Value— Products and Beyond

Anyone can start a business, but if you want to be profitable, you need to stand out. Brand differentiation does not just cover products, pricing, distribution, and the like. You need to stand out by the values you project, a purpose beyond your own wealth, and your ability to personalize customer relationships.

This section will review consumer attitudes that influence choices, what consumers expect from brands beyond products or services purchased, and resources to help you stay on top of ever-growing demands.

> Understanding your brand's 360-degree value for customers

> Meeting customers' elevating expectations for ESG, CSR, personalization, and more

> Defining your brand's purpose and your commitments behind it

A nyone can start a business, but if you want it to be profitable, you need to stand out from a large fray of others. Brand differentiation does not just cover products, pricing, distribution, and the like. You need to stand out by the values you project, a purpose beyond your own wealth, and your ability to build personalized customer relationships en masse.

A brand's "values" go beyond the perception of the value of goods or services for the price paid. Values now cover personal principles, ethics, morals, standards, and such of the founders and leaders. Consumers pay attention to how you treat employees, manage your environmental impact, the authenticity of your messaging, the realization of your promises, and what you do to give back to the communities that give you revenue, distribution, and support. Brands across all categories need to define and build value from 360 degrees, not just a pricing perspective. As an entrepreneur, doing this can be the difference in your success or failure. And this is not likely to change anytime soon. Read on.

What Is Your Brand's 360-Degree Value?

Numerous studies across numerous years show that a brand's values—principles, morals, ethics, sustainability, and more—matter to consumers when it comes to making choices for purchases and loyalty. As of the date of this writing, more than 50 percent of consumers across categories say a brand's values influence their purchasing choices. With all the information in the cyber universe, researching actions that reveal an organization's values is quick and simple and an increasingly present part of many consumers' decision processes.

Per the above, the first step for any new business owner should be to define the values you will project and adhere to and then build your marketing messages, customer experiences, and—very importantly—your partnerships around these values, giving you 360 degrees of authenticity.

Step one as you build your marketing plan is to ask yourself, "What are the values I can practice and offer to my customers beyond what I sell?"

It's tough in any industry to produce and deliver an exclusively unique product. In the age of manufacturing automation where products are produced in record times, if you do come up with a never before seen product, it won't be long before a bigger company replicates it and puts you, a smaller company in catch-up mode. Offering meaningful values beyond product quality can help you stay on course and get ahead.

As you build your business plan and corresponding customer experience and marketing strategies, you need to build out your brand's full circle of values. Your circumference needs to include the following six elements:

1. **Product quality**—How do you provide functional or aesthetic value that supports your price point and secures high satisfaction ratings?

2. **Service quality**—What can you do to assure your customer service team responds and solves problems quickly?

3. **Customer experience**—How can you support the decision process, enhance the trial period, and create events that drive high levels of satisfaction, repeat sales, and referrals?

4. **Emotional value**—We knowingly and unknowingly purchase products and support brands that provide an emotional fulfillment such as security, confidence, status, appreciation, excitement, and so on. What emotional value does your category fulfill, and how does your business do so exceptionally through your products and customer interactions?

5. **Social value**—Customers are demanding more and more social impact on local and national levels from the brands they choose to support, making it imperative for you to deliver ancillary values to the communities that support you. Can you help to further education, health care, equality for gender, age, and ethnicity? How can you engage in programs that help eradicate poverty or child hunger? What other social values like transparency, responsible sourcing, fair hiring practices, or employee rights will you stand behind?

6. **Environmental value**—Entrepreneurs across all industries are being pressured to do capitalism better and that includes putting environmental and social sustainability before profitability. How will you look to lower your carbon and other environmental imprints? Are you committed to produce and distribute products with less resources, less pollution, less toxins, and so on.

You also need to define your CSR (Corporate Social Responsibility) plan, and communicate your ESG (Environmental, Social, and Governance) compliance and policies. Doing so may seem like overkill for an entrepreneur just getting started, but it's not. No matter how large or small you are now or the business category within which you operate, you have to stand for something if you want to succeed. Standing for nothing gets you pretty much nowhere in today's business world. As it should. If you want people to support you, support what matters to them.

Here's some definitions for CSR and ESG to help you get started on mapping out your brand's strategies in these critical areas:

Corporate Social Responsibility—This refers to the impact you have on the community in which you operate. This is not just about the funds you donate to charities. It is about the time you spend furthering programs in place to make life better for others vs. just building your profits. It's about the impact you make on the lives of people beyond your customers. For some good examples of CSR practices and strategies, and how organizations in various industries develop and execute CSR plans, listen to the podcast, *The Caring Economy* by Toby Usnik or read his book of the same title.

ESG—This acronym refers to Environmental, Social, and Governance practices. Companies are judged and patronized according to how well they protect the environment via responsible production and distribution practices, their social activities and treatment of employees, and how they conduct businesses. Examples of ESG activities often monitored by investors and consumers looking for companies with strong values in which to invest or to support include: energy usage and waste reduction, climate change strategy, fair pay and wages for employees, workplace health and benefits for employees, community engagement, corporate governance, ethical business practices, avoidance of conflicts of interest or questionable partnerships, and so on.

Clearly these are commitments you grow as your business develops. Most startups don't have many resources to divert toward doing good as they build product and revenue, however, you can still make an impact by taking a stand for values that matter to you, and volunteering time for programs that support the purpose you establish for your business. The owner of a bookstore in Frisco, Colorado, The Next Page, puts signs in her windows about her support for unjustly banned books, diversity, people of all lifestyles and backgrounds, and hires accordingly. People embrace her values and her store, paying more for her books than they would online because they believe in and want to be associated with her values. As Lisa Holenko, owner of The Next Page, says, "Doing the right thing always pays off. We're fortunate to be part of a community that agrees!"

Charitable donations and/or volunteerism, no matter how small, help showcase your CSR commitments. You don't have to save the world year one of your business, but you do have to do something if you want to attract the 80 percent and higher of consumers that choose brands according to what they do for the greater good. Include storefront signs or messages on your digital sites that state the organizations you support. Donations to the Humane Society, local pet adoptions, childhood cancer research groups, food pantries, your presence in the volunteer lines, and more say a lot about who you are as an entrepreneur and help draw like-minded people to your brand.

Establishing Your Tangible Values

Your tangible values are those that are related to products and services delivered and corresponding transactions, both of which can be measured easily by your customers. Following is a list of tangible values for you to consider.

Price: How you price your product largely defines the perceived value of what you sell. Luxury prices are a good example. A cotton T-shirt might cost you $15 at a retailer like Target and $50–$80 at one like Ralph Lauren. At Gucci, one that bears their logo is priced at $590 as of this writing (no typo here).

If you are producing luxury goods, you will want to price accordingly to compete in this category. Keep in mind you need to earn high prices with your branding and positioning strategies and execution vs. starting out with a similar price tag as Gucci. And also keep in mind that your goods need to project the level of luxury your price reflects in order for you to succeed. I once met a team of entrepreneurs who wanted to start a luxury fashion company. They launched their brand with products with similar prices being charged by recognized luxury brands. However, their brand was unknown and their products did not reflect the distinction or quality of others in the luxury accessory category. They failed as customers were not willing to pay a huge price that was not earned. If you are starting out, create a pricing model that makes it easy for people to try your brand. This will help you identify your best customers, establish a solid customer base and brand recognition, and enable you to introduce other options for pricing as you grow.

Adding price flexibility into your revenue model so you can reward current customers with price incentives for repeat purchases and spark trial among new customers with special price offers can help you add value to your brand. Much more on pricing later on.

Convenience: With e-commerce and online customer service access, convenience is no longer a compelling competitive advantage. Or at least not like it used to be. If you are an e-commerce business, you are always open. Where you can add convenience is by offering live chat for extended hours and detailed answers to frequently asked questions for the all-night shopping sprees or customers that want help now, even if it's 3 a.m. If your business is more physical than online, it still pays off to operate hours that are convenient for your shoppers, not just your payroll. If you cater to adults, offer hours that work for working adults who need time to shop after work, or after picking up kids or pets from daycare. You can also offer other conveniences like curbside pick up, home delivery and more. Keep in mind these conveniences are nice to offer but not likely to be a game changer as many customers will opt to get out of their car and walk into your store if you offer greater value than someone who will deliver to cars in the parking lot.

Quality: As any product or service in any category will fail if expectations for industry standards are not met, competing with promises of superior quality is not the advantage it once was considered to be. Largely because quality is and always will be defined by the consumer, not the producer, and touting your superiority is not likely to be believed, especially in a market with increasing consumer skepticism. Quality standards are expected and promises of superior quality without a distinct definition are trite, cliché, way over used, and not likely to be credible now or in the future. With all the options purchasers across categories have, one bad product experience is all it takes to switch brands. And switching is easier than ever for most business categories. How can you assure your product or service quality is consistent time and time again, and worth customers referring to others? For one, you can set up quality assurance processes for product development and customer service, and regularly ask customers for feedback to know if you are in line. Or not.

Experience: Maya Angelou sums up the most important deliverable for any business.

"I've learned that people will forget what you said, people will forget what you did, but people will never forget how you made them feel."

It is those "feelings" that bring us back for more, for both B2C and B2B purchases. As you build a plan for your business, you cannot ignore the experiences you will offer beyond the products or services sold, and how those experiences will create feelings of happiness, relief, confidence, excitement, status, and so on, all of which create trial and ultimately loyalty. When you make people feel valued and confident about their ability to achieve their personal and professional aspirations, you can more easily take price, and often competitors, out of the equation for your business's long-term success.

Personalization: At one time, personalization referred mostly to including customers' names and transaction details in a direct marketing letter's copy and graphics. Now it is all about building personalized communications, offers, transactions, and experiences. Marketing technology is built and will continue to be built around hyper personalization. As you create your business plan and marketing programs, you need to keep an eye focused on personalizing all aspects of lead nurturing and loyalty. The key to successful personalized marketing you can keep up with is a solid CRM system, like HubSpot or Salesforce. A robust CRM system will allow you to personalize various aspects of your customer communications, view customer data and history quickly so your support team can have personalized conversations, and create automated email campaigns, and schedule sequences specific to individuals relationship with your brand.

Building the Value That Builds Bonds: Purpose

As mentioned earlier, building a sustainable business requires much more than just developing an innovative product or service that fills a real need for a target customer group. Successful startups are often built around purpose. Customers look to do business with brands that support a meaningful and needed purpose beyond their own profitability, and do so with openness, transparency, and authenticity.

In fact, recent Deloitte research shows companies built around a purpose grow three times faster than non-purpose driven competitors. *Inc.* magazine puts out an annual Purpose Power Index listing the top 100 purposeful brands, surveying U.S. customers about how they perceive the power of purpose for 200 brands across 50 industries. Seventh Generation, TOMS, and Zoom were 2022's Top 3.

Important to note is that the data partner for the Purpose Power Index, Dynata, found that 85 million U.S. consumers are motivated to purchase from brands that have purpose, and 149 million will boycott a brand if they don't agree with their sociopolitical purposes or stances on issues. Enough said.

An exemplary brand that is helping to redefine purpose through conscious capitalism is Cotopaxi, which markets Gear for Good and was built around purpose. Founder Davis Smith grew up in Ecuador where he witnessed severe poverty on a daily basis. After starting a successful company selling pool tables made of environmentally sustainable products, he set out to create a company focused on fighting poverty. His vision was to blend his love for nature, adventure, and purpose with outdoor apparel and a foundation focused on giving 1 percent of his company's revenue to nonprofits engaged in poverty alleviation. To further validate his commitment to the purpose he defined for Cotopaxi, he went through the rigorous process of becoming a B Corporation, which requires companies to meet criteria in five key categories, including environmental and social impact. In just a few short years, Cotopaxi became a key competitor in its category, and achieved more than $100 million in revenue.

Following Davis's path is not essential to every entrepreneur's success, but it does show the power of purpose. Consumers want to get behind brands that do good in the world. As an entrepreneur, you need to define what you stand for, what social issues you seek to remedy, and how you will serve the communities which support you.

According to Davis, building a brand around a sustainable purpose takes patience. As he tells it, his first 10 years in business were very frustrating as he tried too quickly to build out his purpose. He soon realized he needed to build a successful business in order to be a successful philanthropist. Taking a step backward to focus on his business skills set his brand up for its current success and sustainable giving.

Tips he shares with entrepreneurs starting a brand today include:

1. Define your purpose and then build your business practices to support that purpose. Just making donations, even small ones, as you start out defines your values to your customers and helps you gain needed support.

2. Build a brand around something you believe in. When the purpose is part of your personal DNA, it's easier to achieve what you desire and make your actions believable.

3. Start small while dreaming big. You cannot do it all at once so don't try. Building both your product and purpose at a sustainable pace builds credibility with customers and investors.

4. Build partnerships to expand your purpose and consequentially your network, visibility, and customer base.

5. Don't be so heads down on your business goals that you don't look up to see what you can do for others. When purpose is part of your business DNA and is not a separate endeavor, you will substantially increase your chances of long-term success.

Davis did not start changing the world the day he opened the doors for his business. He started small but always kept his big dream at the forefront of his mind. Cotopaxi, from the very beginning, made donations to nonprofits working to eradicate poverty. Small, but they helped, and those donations helped Smith put a stake in the ground for his business which now donates 1 percent of its revenue each year to organizations focused on this critical cause. With $100 million in annual sales in 2022, that 1 percent is $1 million, which is no small amount for the organizations and people it benefits.

Building your business around purpose does not have to be a complicated or expensive process. It just has to be. And your purpose does not have to apply to all the customer groups you target and serve. It just needs to be *relevant* to what you do, and your promises and actions around it *authentic*. Additionally, you need to stand by your *commitment*, in all ways, at all times.

Being Relevant, Authentic, and Committed

Relevant

A purpose that aligns with the value you offer customers and society at large is more likely to resonate with your customers than one that seems to be out in left field, or out of the ballpark altogether. If you are an optometrist, supporting programs that provide recycled or new eyewear to underprivileged people is a relevant cause. Aligning your brand with furthering tattoo artistry or organic lavender farms, not so much. Purposes that align with your area of expertise or your personal stories and experiences are more likely to seem actionable and real to your customer groups and gain their support. So will a focus on larger social needs like helping to make housing, education, or healthcare more accessible to all as these issues affect people in and outside of your customer group.

Authentic

Saying you care about an issue when your actions indicate otherwise not only breaks trust in your brand, it can break your brand altogether. There's plenty of research that states consistently over the years, trust is the number one reason consumers or B2B purchasers switch brands. As it's human nature to want to do business with brands and people we trust, this is not likely to change. Ever.

Greenwashing is a good example of inauthentic promises around purpose. Companies that claim to operate toward carbon neutrality or engage in practices that prevent other environmental damage such as water contamination, but can't prove any impact are not just setting themselves up for broken trust and lost customers and revenue, they are setting themselves up for lawsuits. As of this writing, airlines and other companies are facing legal action from customers that felt duped about fake ESG claims. Even those big brands with deep legal pockets that could win these unprecedented lawsuits have a lot more to lose when it comes to customer respect, trust, acquisition, and loyalty scores.

Commitment

Making a single donation to an organization focused on your brand's purpose is not going to cut it. Anyone can donate funds to charity. The kind of purpose consumers want to rally behind are long-lasting commitments to make real and sustainable change that involves time and other resources beyond just donated funds. Going back to Cotopaxi, Davis Smith shows commitment to his purpose of eradiating poverty by donating a percentage of revenue, allocating staff time to serving organizations in the developing countries he supports with his charitable donations, and through a foundation he set up that raises funds from customers and others to further support the causes he has built his brand purpose around.

As an entrepreneur or leader of an established brand it's not about just the money you give, but the commitment you make to foster real change for a real societal need. Your ongoing commitment is what consumers look for, not just the press release about your donation or time-limited promoion to donate a share of proceeds to a cause. For example, if you have a personal connection to Alzheimer's, volunteer your time, tell your stories, and donate goods or proceeds to prevent others from living out similar experiences.

Your purpose can be unrelated to a societal issue, and simply built around spreading joy and personal goodwill as well. Panera, a restaurant chain with locations in the U.S. and Canada known for its fresh baked goods, started out in St. Louis, Missouri, with the goal of bringing out the best in people by providing good food in a warm, welcoming space. This is their guiding purpose. Building on this vision, Panera started a non-profit organization to support local communities, and customers.

Here's a few of the commitments to community and employees Panera fulfills and promotes on posters in its stores:

> ❭ Educational scholarships are available for employees.

> ❭ Each café adopts a family in need of Christmas gifts and food each season.

> ❭ Staff at each café volunteer hours of service toward causes in their local communities.

> ❭ Instead of tossing unsold baked goods in the dumpsters out back of their cafes, or selling day-old breads and pastries for a discount, their cafes donate daily leftovers to local food banks and churches.

> ❭ If a staff member is facing a catastrophic situation, Panera offers assistance.

All of these "acts of kindness" are affordable, easy to execute repeatedly, and deliver a lot of currency for brand respect, sales, and loyalty. As mentioned throughout this chapter, consumers feel good about doing business with businesses that do good.

Just building a product, pushing it through distribution channels and advertising its availability is no longer a formula for success.

While you don't need to start a movement that you may or may not be able to sustain, you need to decide the values your organization will reflect and execute via your CSR activities and ESG behavior.

Consider finding opportunities to support the communities that support you—customer segments, physical locations in which you operate or house your headquarters, and elements of society that reflect your values—underserved, underprivileged people, animal services, education, and so on. You get to decide, but you need to align with something bigger than you and your profitability goals.

Create a plan that keeps your purpose front and center, and actions aligned. Remember, your purpose should be relevant to your brand and leadership stories, your actions authentic and not "washed" in any way, and you must show commitment at all levels of your organization, not just a donation or company volunteer day once in a while that you post about on social media.

GO TIME

You've done the hard part: crafted an idea that you are ready to execute as a real business. Now is the time to identify your brand purpose and outline your commitments around that purpose to make it real for your team and customers. Below are some questions to get you started. Start an Excel spreadsheet, label Sheet #1 Branding (you'll be adding to this later) and document answers to the following. Later, you will build marketing programs around these answers, as they are today, and how they may evolve over time.

1. What is a societal need associated with your product that you can credibly support? One that customers can easily connect to your business and offerings? Identify one that matters to you, and is aligned with your category or you personally, and list this as your purpose. At least for now. As society changes, so too can and should brands.

2. What organizations exist that support the purpose you defined in action item 1? How can you affordably support one or several of these organizations with the resources you have? What kind of impact can you have by volunteering your time, allocating staff time and services, and so on? List examples of organizations you can explore for a good fit in your Excel spreadsheet.

3. How will you communicate your support to customers, communities, and others in ways that are not self-serving? Can you use your social pages, and encourage employees to do the same, to promote your purpose and engage others appropriately?

4. What opportunities exist for you to involve your communities, customers, business partners or suppliers, and more in your cause? How can you do so in ways that also introduces your business at the same time?

Document ideas that you can refine and build actions upon. You're now on your way to setting up your brand to rise above some of the challenges startups face today.

CHAPTER 2

Know Your Markets and Customers

To win at any game—business or sports—you need to understand the market in which you are playing, how your customers make choices, and all you can about your competition so you can score and dominate the playing field before they do.

You also need to understand the trends, attitudes, and purchasing criteria that influence your customers, and their influencers. Loyalty is often assigned to brands whose value to customers goes beyond the products and services sold. Knowing what matters to consumers and what may cause them to switch from another brand to your brand, and vice versa, is critical to growing sales, retaining customers and revenue, and setting your business up for sustainable growth.

This chapter will review what you should know about your:

> Marketplace

> Market and economic indicators

> Consumer attitudes that impact choice

> Consumer trust and confidence

Know Your Markets

Knowing What You Don't Know You Don't Know

One of the most dangerous behaviors for entrepreneurs in any business sector is to assume. Assume you know the market in which you are operating, assume you know your customers' attitudes toward your business category, assume you know why your customers choose one brand over another, and what they like about your business. Assume your customers are "just like you." And a lot more.

Assumptions are almost always wrong. Case in point: Mitt Romney and Hillary Clinton assumed they had easy presidential victories ahead, largely based on erroneous polls, and neither were prepared to deliver a concession speech when the time came for them to do just that.

Brands that operate on assumptions often cease to exist. Remember the typewriter? When personal computers started to evolve, many typewriter companies assumed it would just be a trend and that consumers would always prefer a typewriter over a slow, cumbersome computer that needed a printer to produce an actual document. So instead of reinventing to keep up with technologies, they assumed the status quo was the future. Where are those companies now? There are also many products successful brands failed to launch by assuming consumers would want them. Remember Google Glass, the glasses with a heads-up computer screen?

The good news is that with all the information available about consumer purchasing trends, attitudes, expectations of brands; market dynamics and influences, economic indicators, and growth projections for regional and national economies and business categories, you can find just about any data you need to make "informed" decisions about how to market your business. The keyword here is "informed" decisions. Spending money, time, and energy on marketing just because you can is not just silly, but a formula for earning a tombstone in that infamous cemetery of dead brands.

Before you start any kind of marketing program, you need to gather a lot of information about what you don't know you don't know. Regardless of how well you know your industry, or at least assume you do, there's a lot you need to learn, primarily because reality in all business sectors changes often and quite often dramatically, just like the weather or the affection of your cat or pet bird.

No matter your business category, there are various groups compiling data about businesses like yours, your customers, market opportunities, market risks, and other nuggets of information you need to move forward effectively and efficiently. Much of the needed information is available without expensive subscriptions, and quite often free of charge or the commitment to do a sales demo.

Looking Below the Surface of Your Marketplace

While free information is available for just about any industry, for the sake of simplicity, let's look at the insurance sector.

If you are in the process of starting a new independent business or opening a franchise, you should know if the market you intend to serve is growing or shrinking. Googling "insurance market projections" brings up many credible resources.

For me, the first result out of more than 87 million results was a report from Swiss Re, done in April 2023, that shows the return on equity, or ROE, for U.S. property and casualty insurance to be better in 2023 than it was in 2022 due to higher premium rates and investment yield. This same report forecasts premium rates to grow by 7.5 percent in 2023 and 5.5 percent in 2024. This information suggests that entrepreneurs just getting started in this industry should consider ramping up marketing in 2023 to lock in higher premium rates and higher profits. Profits generated during this time period of potentially higher revenue can help maintain funding for 2024 marketing if revenues fall per the projected 2 percent decline in premium rates.

Another report by McKinsey shows health insurance continued to be the fastest-growing type of insurance with a 5.9 percent growth in 2019, and that it accounted for approximately 25 percent of all insurance premiums worldwide in 2019. Statista shows forecasts for the global health insurance market from 2021 to 2026 to grow by around $3 billion. Note to anyone considering launching a business in this sector.

If you change the search to just cover U.S. insurance market projections, you might find a report by Grand View Research showing that the US individual health insurance market is expected to grow by more than 6 percent from 2023 to 2030. This information shows that while health insurance is growing at a slightly slower rate than property and casualty insurance in 2023, it is projected to maintain a solid growth rate for the next 7 years, suggesting more sustainable growth and revenue streams. Paying attention to studies and projections for your industry over short-term and long-term time periods will help you align your marketing efforts and spend with market opportunities and risks, and plan accordingly for product development, budgeting, funding needs, and more.

Clearly, a growth industry and local market is a good indication that there is room for your business to enter and compete, and that your marketing efforts have a fair chance of paying off. If you see a steady decline in your industry area, you will want to explore why, and what a stagnant or shrinking market might mean for your short-term and long-term plans. Some questions to consider:

> Is your category being morphed by another?

> Is new technology replacing the status quo?

> Is consumer demand for your product growing or shrinking due to functional alternatives or changes in lifestyle?

> Are consumers spending less due to changing needs, values, a shaky job market?

> Are environmental and supply chain issues impeding operational processes and forcing price changes that could hurt startups?

A good example of how quickly markets can change is the growing use of automation and robotics in manufacturing. These technologies improve operational outcomes such as lower cost of production per unit, greater efficiencies, and faster times to market. As established brands invest in automation technologies, the barrier to entry is more difficult as small brands that cannot afford these systems cannot produce as quickly and meet marketing and customer expectations as easily as those with these advantages. Another example is the role of AI in marketing and what this means for copywriters, graphic designers, and content producers, and of course brands needing these services. If you are starting a marketing consultancy or graphic design business, how can you compete with AI platforms that automatically build design and content elements based on a few keywords. How can you position yourself as better than robotic outputs to customers who see these tools as lower cost options for the work you provide?

On the flip side, if your category is growing rapidly, you will want to adapt your GTM (Go To Market) plan accordingly. Can you quickly get the funding or other resources you need to ride a current wave of revenue potential to set you up for business growth or even expansion into new markets sooner than maybe originally planned?

Keeping a pulse on your markets will help you project peaks and valleys in sales and manage your marketing and other resources accordingly. Keep in mind that even the most clever marketing campaigns, personalized promotions, and pricing plans won't bring you sales if no one wants your product any more, or has the means or mindset to purchase it. It's also important to always market from a growth mindset, but to also manage marketing resources against current circumstances. Operating with growth in mind instead of fear of failure is the difference between companies that rise above difficult times and those that do not.

Companies that put out information about growth projections and consumer behavior trends affecting multiple industries, often for free, include:

❯ Major accounting firms—PwC, Deloitte, EY

❯ Market research firms—Forrester, IpSos, Edelman DXI, Kantar, Gartner

❯ Global consulting firms—McKinsey, Bain, Boston Consulting Group, KMPG

❯ Information Services—NeilsenIQ, Statista, IBISWorld

❯ Financial companies—Dun & Bradstreet, Bloomberg, MarketWatch

❯ Government sites—SBA (Small Business Administration), FTC, and others with government data

Another solid resource for keeping a pulse on any market is to review press release distribution sites. Businesses post news about earnings, growth, product releases, and more daily on these sites. Browsing press releases from industry players and leaders can help you stay on top of new developments and growing companies with whom you may compete or potentially partner with at some point. Leading newswire sites include PR Newswire/CISION, Business Wire, and Global News Wire.

What You Can Learn from Wall Street and Other Economic Indicators

Watching stocks in your industry offers another timely indicator of market dynamics. Stocks prices go up and down due to many factors but from a marketing lens you can gauge activity that might impact the ROI of your marketing efforts. When category leaders' stocks rise or fall, pay attention as to why. Rising stock prices could indicate growing demand for your category while falling prices might indicate the opposite. Declining stock prices can also set up take overs of lower performing companies and elevated merger and acquisition activity, both of which can impact competitive landscapes and pricing of goods and services as bigger companies with greater economies of scale gain control of markets. If you have to add more value or lower your price to compete for new customers and loyalty among existing customers due to accelerated M&A activity in your space, you will likely need to change your marketing approach and budget accordingly.

Monitoring Marketing Channel Reports

Associations for your industry as well as associations representing the marketing industry in general are valuable to join or at least follow. They often put out reports on consumer and business trends and shed light on best practices for given industries. Associations and other groups study how businesses spend advertising resources across channels, which channels best engage consumers in various B2B and B2C industries, and how different generations use and react to different channels. These are important to monitor as you develop your own marketing budgets and priorities.

Paying attention to the channels your target audiences use the most for socializing with others online or for gathering information about the decisions they make will help you avoid costly mistakes, like putting all your money into Facebook ads when your most valuable prospects use TikTok or Instagram instead.

Monitoring ad spending among big brands in your categories will help you see where you should be putting your resources as well. Category leaders often spend a lot of money and time monitoring the channels most used daily for socializing and for shopping by those spending the most on products you both sell. You can learn at their expense by paying attention to where they are most present.

Channel studies often indicate which mediums drive the most engagement and sales and by which consumers. For example, Gen Z, Gen X, Millennials, and Boomers spend differently, use different channels to gather information, and they respond to marketing activities differently as well. Millennials to Boomers tend to value personalized emails more than other generations while Gen Z is heavily influenced by creators on TikTok and Instagram.

A good source for helping you plan your time and budget resources for marketing programs is the Winterberry Group's annual outlook report on advertising spend across channels and industries. Their reports provide valuable insights into where big brand competitors are putting their marketing dollars. Chances are high big brands in your space have done enough testing and vetting to determine which channels pay off and which are a waste of money. Monitoring how the big players in your industry are spending their money can help you avoid costly mistakes and prioritize the channels that are paying off the most, at least for the moment.

Winterberry predicted in their "Outlook for Advertising, Marketing and Data 2024 Report," a year-over-year (YOY) growth of online spending of 14.9 percent reflecting a total spend of $368.8 billion and a 4.1 percent increase in offline advertising to a total of $203 billion. Note that some of this projected growth is due to political events happening in 2024. Specific areas of growth predicted in this Outlook 2024 report show a 12.4 percent increase in search ad spend, 13.8 percent for email/SMS/push, 16.6 percent for video, 30.4 percent for Connected TV (ads in music and video streams), and 16.1 percent for display ads.

As an entrepreneur just starting out and with a low marketing budget, reports on media spend for your category and in general can provide insight on how you can best use your resources to create visibility for your brand, and drive prospective purchasers, to your digital assets to start conversations, and ultimately journeys to sales conversion.

Companies that frequently share channel usage, engagement, and sales reports include:

> Nielsen

> Insider Intelligence

> Winterberry Group

> Associations such as ANA—Association of National Advertisers

Note: Groups that monitor channel usage, ads, engagement, and sales conversions merge and change branding often. Google what you want to learn and view various reports to get the best view of your consumers at any given time.

Paying Attention to Technology Updates

In addition to all of the above, you also need to stay on top of technological developments in your space, as difficult as it may seem in a world that seems to be moving at the speed of light, and at times, even faster. Monitoring current developments such as how new technology like robotics or AI impact the perceived value of your product category and sales trends is key to knowing if you are developing at the pace of the market or falling behind. This is especially critical if you are in the software business or another rapidly changing technology sector. If you don't have the resources to scale your product development quickly, you will have a hard time competing with others in your sector, large or small, regardless of how brilliant your marketing execution may be. Companies that can't develop new features quickly risk launching a product that is one, two, or more years behind the market leaders when they finally complete their first product release. This results in failing to meet customer expectations when new releases don't keep up with what others are offering. Not a formula for success for any type of software in any industry. If you are in an industry that changes rapidly, you need to secure financial resources to ramp up quickly in order to launch in ways that set you up for sales or to be purchased by a bigger player in your industry if that is your goal.

If you can't operate fast enough to keep up with industry developments, you may need to consider targeting a small niche that needs a few of the features you are developing and put a stake in that pond instead of the bigger ocean initially. For startups, starting with a small focus in order to build revenue and work out any bugs or kinks in a product before jumping onto a bigger stage is often what sets successes apart from failures. Currently, 95 percent of startups fail, often by trying to do too much too soon. Don't set yourself up to be among these statistics.

If you operate in a rapidly evolving industry like software and don't have the intention or resources to take over your world, you need to have your exit plan in mind when you enter the market. Are you building a new feature you hope to sell to the market leaders, like a Microsoft or Adobe, and if so, what is the time frame for your new feature to be and remain relevant, and thus attractive to potential companies wanting to grow by acquisition? If this is your plan, your marketing activities will want to focus on the innovation and profitability associated with your features and tease what future generations could look like as well.

As you put together your Do-It-Yourself Marketing plan, document the resources for market insights that you can access easily and affordably, create a digital dashboard that contains these resources, and schedule time each week to review them.

Know Your Customers

Gaining a solid and accurate understanding of what moves customers to behavior, brand and product choices, and ultimately loyalty is critical to any successful marketing plan. To really hit the jackpot for Return On Marketing Investment (ROMI) you need to know your customers from various angles, including:

- ≫ The level of trust they have in your brand category
- ≫ The value of products, services, and experiences they expect from your brand
- ≫ Which emotions, aspirations, fears, and needs drive engagement and behavior

Understanding the Complexity of Trust

Monitoring the level of consumer trust in your business category is a great place to start. If consumers don't trust the industry in which you operate, you may have a hard time getting them to trust the promises and claims you make in your marketing campaigns about your product and service quality. There is a lot of information about consumers' level of trust in businesses, what categories they trust the most and least, what brand values and actions build or break trust, and even how influencers of trust change across political affiliation.

Because reports on trust cover various aspects of trust, it's important to review multiple studies vs. taking the one-and-done approach. Below are summaries of two different aspects of trust.

Edelman Trust Barometer 2023 report focused on how trust is influenced by elements such as a brand's sensitivity to consumer vulnerabilities, health and environmental impact, position on social issues, and even spokespersons delivering brand messaging.

• • • • •

PwC conducts surveys for its annual Consumer Intelligence Series and includes trust as a key focus. Their 2022 report covered levels of trust for brands among consumers and employees, how to build trust for both groups, which industries are trusted the most or least, and the gap between actual consumer trust for a brand and the perceived level of trust among executions.

This same PwC report shares the following example of how out of touch business executives, including entrepreneurs, can be about consumers trust in their business category and brand.

87 percent of business executives think customers trust them when in reality only around 30 percent of their customers actually do.

An inherent danger in such a jarring misperception is that these and other reports on trust show a solid majority of 71 percent of consumers say they are unlikely to purchase from a brand that has lost their trust.

The good news is that you can find reports about trust trends in just about every industry quickly with online searches. Look deep to discover how trust can vary among the different generations and demographics you serve; how current social, political, and even category events and issues may change perceptions of trustworthiness for brands in your industry, and so on.

Meeting Audience and Individual Brand Expectations

It's a given that customers expect value in the goods and services they purchase that is at least equal to the price they paid. But today, and likely forever more, there are other definitions of value they expect. These values include the CSR and ESG scores mentioned in Chapter 1, which sum up your actions for corporate social responsibility, environmental and social practices, and governance of your employees and other constituents. Consumers have many choices now and many of those choices go toward companies that put time, energy, and money behind the values they profess to have.

As also discussed in Chapter 1, a brand's values are closely aligned with their purpose, and having a purpose beyond profits is critical to securing sales and customer loyalty. An article published in 2022 by *Forbes*, states that consumers are four to six times more likely to shop from purpose-driven brands. Values beyond those aligned with purpose also unfold with day-to-day routine activities. For example, responsible practices that get consumers' attention include lowering energy consumption in your workplace, paying employees' fair wages, and directly visible actions like using paper bags, eliminating single-use plastic straws and other materials from your stores, and more.

Little random acts of responsible operations and employee management that show your values toward the earth and your employees can go a long way. Studies from various groups show that between 70–90 percent of consumers will boycott brands that cross the boundaries they set for the companies they choose to patronize. These boundaries set the standard for what is acceptable for employee wages, unfair business practices, charitable support, and full transparency about a company's financials. On the flip side, many studies show as much as 80 percent of consumers will make repeat purchases and refer others to brands that meet their expectations for product quality and CSR.

In addition to high demands for brands to live up to expected social and political values, consumers have increasing high demands for service and personalization.

Here's some data from various recent reports on the role of customer service and personalized attention for driving consumer choices:

❯ Customers want personalized brand experiences and communications. Per an Epsilon study, 80 percent are more likely to purchase from a brand that personalizes communications and offers.

❯ Statista shows that more than 60 percent of consumers will switch brands or diminish loyalty due to a lack of personalization.

❯ Statista also shows that 40 percent of customers stopped patronizing a given brand due to bad customer service and that $75 billion dollars is lost annually from customer churn across categories.

❯ Per responsive customer service, a June 2022 report by Statista shows that 70 percent expect a response to an inquiry the same day, 46 percent the next day, and roughly only 16 percent are willing to wait 3 days for a customer service reply.

❯ Salesforce Research showed 89 percent of consumers say a positive brand experience will make them more likely to purchase from a given brand again.

Consumers also state they want a phygital experience. Not a typo but a new aspect of the customer experience entrepreneurs across categories in B2B and B2C sectors cannot ignore. Phygital refers to experiences that blend both digital and in-person interaction. QR codes are an example. You scan a code in a physical environment such as a trade show, a restaurant, or retail center which then directly engages you with a brand via its digital assets. Other examples include live interaction with chatbots, and augmented reality that allows you to experience a brand's products in a digital setting before making a decision to interact in a physical setting such as a retail store or event.

As an entrepreneur, you need to build your brand around these and other expectations of your customers. While it might seem overwhelming, the plethora of marketing technology that is available, and at affordable price points, makes it possible for small business owners to deliver the same kind of personalized marketing and customer experiences as many bigger competitors.

Addressing Emotional Expectations

Appealing to the psychology of choice is the foundation of all successful marketing. Gerald Zaltman, a Harvard business professor, neuromarketing pioneer, and author that studied consumer behavior and purchasing choices, was among the first to conclude from years of research that at least 90 percent of the choices we make are governed by the unconscious mind. This suggests that promises of convenience, lowest price and best quality don't drive behavior as much as tapping the triggers deep within our human psyches. The unconscious triggers of behavior, consumer and otherwise, are related to what I call Survival DNA. Realized or not, most of what we humans do is rooted in our need to survive or thrive physically, socially, emotionally, spiritually, and the like.

Regardless of what you are marketing and to whom, not understanding the elements of survival associated with your product category will seriously limit your ability to engage consumers in conversations and convert leads to loyal customers. Consider the following.

Purchasing luxury items is completely unnecessary for our physical survival, yet the luxury sector of retail continues to thrive. A forecast prepared by Bain & Co. and Italy's luxury association, Altagamma, show global luxury sales to reach $360–$380 billion EUROS, roughly $405 billion USD, in 2023, up between 5–12 percent from 2022. In the U.S. alone, the luxury market is expected to be worth $126 billion by 2026. According to *eMarketer*, sales for luxury goods between 2022 and 2026 are expected to increase by 17 percent, which reflects a 5.6 percent annual growth rate. All for items that are essentially unnecessary as their function can be replaced by far more practically priced items.

The reality is that luxury goods produce the very same function as non-luxury goods but at a price point exponentially higher, which many consumers are more than willing to overpay. Back to the example of the basic white T-shirt. A white cotton T-shirt is simply a staple for many wardrobes, worn alone or layered with other apparel; worn for daily activities such as working out, covering up on the beach, and so on. Yet the options and price ranges for something this simple all over the spectrum, e.g., the $15 to $590 price range mentioned earlier. Gucci sells a washed 100 percent cotton jersey T-shirt for $590, complete with the Gucci logo. Eddie Bauer sells a 100 percent cotton T-shirt for closer to $30 with its logo. The fabric is the same, the function identical, the logo and price are the primary differences. So, why does the $590 version of the basic white T-shirt continue to sell? Because it appeals to consumers' survival DNA, which I believe in this case is rooted in a sense of superiority. Few people other than the purchaser know the price paid for that Gucci T-shirt, yet the wearer likely feels, often unconsciously, that their ability to pay that extraordinary price, makes them superior to others which gives them a sense of status, greater self-worth, more extrinsic beauty, social security, and confidence that they have achieved their aspirations in life, or are at least on the path to doing so. Much of marketing is not just about the product function, but how your product and brand make consumers feel.

This whole notion of appealing to survival DNA is an important element of your marketing plan. Are you pricing and positioning your products as functional, practical, aspirational, or "luxurious" per your price and the positioning you convey with your brand iconology and advertising imagery? Your decision is not small as it changes your competitive landscape and how you present your products and brands across all marketing functions. And of course, it changes the universe to whom you market your products. While luxury consumers may represent a higher profit margin as they clamor for that logo on their chest or sleeve, belt buckle or handbag, the volume of this population is simply much, much smaller than the general consumer base. And in many cases their fickleness is much larger. This population can and often changes loyalty with the trends, runway highlights, and the slightest breeze.

Gathering information about your consumers, their survival DNA, and purchasing mindset is actually simple and affordable, and the critical first step toward a successful marketing plan you can count on to build leads and sales, no matter the category within which you operate.

Many of the resources mentioned earlier in this chapter for market reports also produce and distribute information on purchasing projections and consumer attitudes. Look for reports on consumer confidence, spending attitudes, purchasing intent, and more. *Nielsen* puts out annual reports on consumer behavior and trends as do several media organizations including *Forbes*, *Ad Age*, and *Entrepreneur* magazine. Search social media sites such as LinkedIn for reports on consumer behavior and industry trends as well. LinkedIn posts some of its own research as do many members on their business and personal pages.

Making Sense of Data and Acting On It

If you are developing a new pet product, or service such as daycare or grooming, you'll want to take a look at reports on the pet industry for the most recent past year. An example: A 2023 Statista report shows the size of market per pet category, showing the number of households with dogs, cats, fish, birds, reptiles, and horses. If you are targeting dog owners, your total addressable market is more than 65 million while it's only around 6 million if you are trying to reach and sell to households with birds. From this data report, you can also see the trends over the past 10 years for each pet category. This specific example shows that over a two-year period, 2019/2020 to 2021/2022, households owning dogs went from roughly 63 million to 69 million. Interestingly, if you look at Statista's report on owner occupied housing units, you will see that owner occupied housing went up from about 80 million to close to 84 million over this same time period. You can fairly assume that ownership of dogs as pets goes up with ownership of homes. This tells you that as housing markets change, so too can the market or number of potential consumers likely to purchase products for dogs. As an entrepreneur, you may want to increase your inventory, marketing spend and resources when housing sales go up in order to capitalize on a strong market. When interest rates go up or other events that can decrease housing sales, you may want to contract a bit so you don't spend more than the market can return, or end up with idle inventory in costly warehouses that even the birds don't want.

Knowing what is happening or projected to happen in your market, what influences your customers, and other critical elements like your competition, barriers to entry, and the merger and acquisition climate in your category is critical to optimizing efficiencies and marketing return. Making a habit of regularly reviewing market and consumer data will enable you to make wise decisions in real time with current and real data that can help you best manage your resources and funding needs.

GO TIME

❯ Create a worksheet in the Excel file you started per Chapter 1. Use this new sheet to document happenings, trends, projections, mergers and acquisitions, stock market activity for key industry leaders, and such for your marketplace. Add columns for consumer trust and confidence scores in your industry, and more for attitudes and expectations. Consumers are in control, but what that means differs and often changes quickly. Update this sheet often.

❯ Compile a list of companies that regularly report on your industry's status, projections, and trends. Sign up for their newsletters and emails, follow them on social media, and check their websites for new reports so you can better plan for product development, marketing spend, hiring, expansion, and other key activities.

❯ Talk to your customers. Often. Whether it is via live chat, phone interviews, live events, formal surveys using Survey Monkey, HubSpot, or other online tools, engage your customers, and when possible your prospects, in dialogue. Ask questions and listen. Find out what they seek in your category, the changes that interest them, e.g., AI, automation, and other technology breakthroughs. Ask what they like about doing business with you, and what they don't. Dig a bit deeper to understand the emotions that influence them. What fears or anxieties do they anticipate minimizing with products in your category? What aspirations do they expect to achieve and how do they believe your brand can best help them get there? These questions will help you identify what makes them hesitant, what inspires them to invest in their goals and happiness, and what they expect from brands to which they assign their loyalty.

》 Build an ESP table to document and manage your Emotional Selling Propositions. List the ESP that is most influential for engaging prospects and closing business. Is it job security? Is it social acceptance? Actualization or material wealth? No matter what you sell, and what industry in which you operate, there is an emotional value connected to what your business offers. In this ESP table, include a column to list how you will fulfill those emotions, is it via concierge-like personal service, is it exclusivity for your services or products. Once you define your messaging strategies, you can add keywords and visuals to this table to guide execution of your campaigns.

CHAPTER 3

Understanding Real Drivers of Choice

To launch sales for any business in any category, you need to know how to tap into the psychology of choice for purchases in your category. This section covers the fundamentals of behavioral economics critical for every entrepreneur to understand, and social influences that spark emotional reactions and hormonal rushes that drive behavior, including purchases and loyalty.

Learn about the impact of the following elements on consumer behavior and how you can tap into each to build positive relationships and cash flow for your business.

> FOMO—Fear of missing out

> Scarcity

> Authority

> Cognition

> Hormones

The Fundamentals of Behavioral Economics

Gathering information to build a successful marketing plan does not end with compiling data about market and consumer trends. You also need to gain a solid understanding of how your target consumers make decisions about products and brands and assign loyalty. Studying behavioral economics is a good start.

Behavioral economics is the science of studying how psychology, emotions, our cognitive processes, and the nuances of our culture and social constructs influence decisions we make. Theories are built upon the premise that we humans make more irrational decisions than we do rational ones. Consumers may plan to do rational things, like eat healthy and exercise daily to get in or stay in shape, to stay on a study schedule to meet school deadlines and get good grades, and so on. But distractions that appeal to our emotions, our cognition or perceptions, and our inherent need to achieve satisfaction from choices we make often sideline rational judgement and lead to decisions that disrupt our intentions.

Marketing needs to address the ups and downs, ins and outs, good and bad of decision making. Some products we sell are designed to keep consumers on that rational path, others to deviate from well-planned routines, and others to experience unexpected moments of joy. No matter what you sell, the diet plan or the double chocolate caramel drizzle cheesecake, you need to understand the complexities of decision making that apply to humans everywhere, in all categories, B2B and business to consumer B2C.

As a business owner or operator, you need to tap into human behavior to engage customers with your brand, your messages and promises, and your products or services. To influence sales, customer loyalty, and business growth, you must influence consumer behavior. It's that simple. Yet the complexity is that, according to research cited before, much of our thoughts influencing our behavior are driven by our unconscious mind.

Behavioral economics presents many insights about how we unconsciously make choices that do not align with classic economical theory, which states that we make choices based on analyzing which decisions will lead to the greatest satisfaction of goals and needs most efficiently. Knowing the triggers of the unconscious mind is key to engaging consumers and influencing behavior. Current scientists of our time sharing the most valuable concepts about behavioral triggers for marketers include Robert Cialdini, author of *Influence: The Psychology of Persuasion,* and *Pre-Suasion: A Revolutionary Way to Influence and Persuade*; Dan Ariely who wrote *Predictably Irrational: The Hidden Forces That Shape Our Decisions*; and the late Daniel Kahneman, a Nobel prize winner and author of *Thinking, Fast and Slow.* These and other psychologists conducted studies to see how we humans respond to influences like FOMO, scarcity, herd mentality or social proof, and a lot of other elements of behavior. As a marketer for your business, you need to understand which behavioral economics concepts apply most to the decisions made for your business category and include appropriate appeals and solutions in your content and experiences.

The following are some theories powerful to the point that you cannot ignore them.

Social Motivators You Need to Address

FOMO: The Fear of Missing Out

The fear of missing out is one of the most powerful, and often unconscious, influencers of the not so rational decisions we make. Whether we realize it or not, or most importantly are willing to admit it or not, we don't want to miss out on what others have or are experiencing. Missing out makes us feel inferior and vulnerable to losing the survival game should the world end tomorrow. FOMO applies to just about all aspects of our lives, no matter who we are or what we do. People choose products that everyone else seems to have to equalize status, achievement, and functional abilities. For example, when you see an athlete cross the finish line in a new brand of running shoes, you may be suddenly inspired to trade your current shoes in for what you now might perceive as a superior shoe so you can up your own performance. If a business competitor has a social media consultant to help them rank higher in SEO searches, you might suddenly feel compelled to hire your own consultant when in reality you can do it yourself (as you will learn later on in this book). And if everyone is waiting in the rain to get into a doughnut shop you've never heard of, there's a chance you might jump in line to avoid missing out on something others enjoy. We are wired to seek what others have so that we can equalize playing fields and set ourselves up to succeed or just enjoy the same things that appear to bring others joy. When you discover through researching consumer attitudes and behavior trends, and talking to prospects and customers about what they fear is missing in their lives as it relates to your category, your marketing will be far more effective.

Scarcity

Like FOMO, scarcity is a highly influential driver of our behavior. Everywhere we look we see attempts to create urgency and get us to buy something sooner than later such as airline tickets and hotel rooms with just "1 left at this price," and "limited time" offers. And although we soon find there are many more than only one ticket left at that price, and the promotion lasts longer than stated, we often still respond just in case its true. If so, we might miss out on something that others might have that we do not, reinforcing the influences of social proof and FOMO. As stated before, we are largely driven by our survival DNA which makes us purchase items that make us feel less vulnerable, like huge amounts of food storage in case of famine, war, or alien attacks on our towns and cities. Doing so gives us a sense of safety and assurance that we are poised to survive whatever comes our way because we have something that will soon be scarce. It's no coincidence that so much advertising across categories builds on the scarcity principle.

Making products seem scarce, or limited, is also a common strategy for higher pricing. If we are afraid of losing something we think we need, or we believe we need to be equal to others socially or professionally, we will pay a premium price. Launching a new product with a limited time price offering, or with limited inventory to sell, to justify a high price, can be a good strategy for new businesses wanting to establish prestige and intrigue.

Authority

As we learn from the renowned Milgram study that showed most people will do what people in authority instruct them to do even if it goes against their moral conscience, the presence of authority can be a strong influencer of behavior. This not only applies to the Milgram experiment conducted by psychologist Stanley Milgram and Yale University, it applies to purchasing choices as well. When authorities are cited in industry studies or testimonials about products, we tend to believe their statements and choose products they endorse as we tend to trust people with recognized expertise. Note that "authority" is not always a celebrity or someone whose name is familiar to people in a given industry or community. In fact, endorsements by real people that reflect real customers often go further than endorsements from celebrities that people automatically know were paid to recommend your brand. If you are selling nutrition or health care products, a family physician who is a health authority by education and occupation is a "real" person whose expertise you may want to align with your brand. An amateur athlete benefiting from your nutritional products would be another trusted authority especially for the weekend warriors wanting to up their own games. Examples of authorities you may want to connect to your brand include product developers, innovators of new technology in any given category, authors, educators, and other types of subject matter experts.

Cognition

Aligning with our survival DNA, we humans are wired to fear loss more than we seek rewards. Psychologist Daniel Kahnemann, mentioned earlier, studied this concept known as loss aversion and showed from his research with associate Amos Tversky that losses can have twice the psychological impact as gains. In simpler terms, the pain from a loss can be twice as intense as the joy from gaining a positive outcome. We will pay large amounts of money for insurance to protect us from loss if we get in an automobile accident, experience a fire, earthquake, flood, or other disaster that compromises our homes, health, or businesses. These monthly payments are not about a potential reward but simply avoiding loss. Without realizing it, we recognize and respond to risks before we see opportunities. One of my favorite experiments as a presenter and trainer is to show audiences the optical illusion drawing, *All is Vanity*, by Charles Gilbert. This art presents a double image, one of a woman looking at her reflection in a mirror and the other image a skull. The majority of people viewing this art in my sessions always saw the skull first, and then the woman. This reflects the influence of our survival DNA, which shows us what we need to fear so we can protect ourselves before we seek opportunities beyond preservation. How we respond to stimuli, like this illustration, sounds, and even colors, is also a reflection of our cognition, which is our embedded perceptions that build up over time from experiences and the culture in which we are raised. Studies show that certain colors in one culture may trigger caution or anxiety and quite another effect in another culture.

Knowing how your customers intuitively and unconsciously perceive business and product categories, and what threats and opportunities they associate with yours will help you craft marketing messages and customer experiences of direct relevance. I had a consulting client that was selling real estate investment portfolios at a time when real estate was risky. He would approach prospects with cheerful messages about the potential return from his funds. No one took him seriously and he couldn't get prospects to give him more than a few minutes before ending the conversation. Cognitively, they didn't believe anything he said. Associating real estate with a positive investment return was not something they could do at the time. So we took a completely different approach and started telling them what they believed. "Real estate is risky. You are right to be cautious. We get it." Suddenly they trusted him and wanted to hear more. My client slowly shifted the conversation from risks to opportunities. By talking to the cognitive dissonance that shaped their perceptions and reality, he became a respected authority with potential clients who would not have given him a chance before.

The Role of Hormones

Other drivers of behavior are hormones, or neurotransmitters, which compel us to act when released as a result of certain stimuli. These neurotransmitters interact with receptors throughout our brains to regulate emotions, influence memory, our cognitive function, attention span, cravings, energy, even our appetites.

For marketers, the neurotransmitters that most influence purchasing behavior include dopamine, oxytocin, and cortisol.

Dopamine

Dopamine is the powerful hormone that gives us that euphoric feeling, creates excitement, inspires us to take risks, and can motivate us to act impulsively. It also is associated with reinforcement and rewards. In many cases, we will continue to do whatever released dopamine and made us feel on top of the world, accomplished, attractive, infallible, and the like. Research by Stanford Professor Dr. Robert Sapolsky shows we even experience dopamine when we just anticipate a reward or a positive experience. The whole notion of religion is an example of creating anticipation for a reward that is not tangibly delivered. But the anticipation of that reward creates strong feelings of hope and trust and even joy, and these feelings impact our behavior. Pretty much all mainstream religions promise immense joy in an afterlife if you suffer and obey in this life, but none of those religions literally deliver on that promise as the joy comes after you have left this life and are no longer sitting in their pews once a week. And those preaching the promises of a given faith have not experienced or been an eyewitness to the rewards promised as they are not currently living in that "after life." Think about this for a moment. The power of anticipation is so strong people build their lives around it. What anticipation can you ethically promise in your marketing campaigns and then actually and honestly deliver with your products, services, and commitments? If potential purchasers anticipate success, peace of mind, security, joy or an elevated status in work or society from your product, chances are they are more likely to listen to your promises, and ultimately purchase from you.

We see these attempts to spark dopamine rushes in advertising across all industries. Get rich quick, land that new job, retire early, and other promises are based on the anticipation of rewards we may be seeking. If we eat a certain fast food over another, we will be rewarded with a sensory experience like no other. If we drive a specific overpriced car, we will attract beautiful people, and elevate our social status. You get it.

When you can create customer experiences that make people feel accomplished, successful, recognized, and other rewarding emotions, you not only increase your chance of acquiring new customers, but of maintaining their loyalty and referrals.

Oxytocin

Often referred to as the love hormone, oxytocin is released when we feel connected to another person in a loving way. It sparks those warm, fuzzy feelings we get when we "fall in love," which in turn lowers stress and anxiety and regulates important feelings like trust and empathy. Oxytocin also spurs positive memories and overall feelings of well-being. Like dopamine, many marketing campaigns and programs are designed to spark a rush of this neurotransmitter as it creates feelings that form bonds which are much stronger than the joy of saving a dollar or two on any given purchase. No matter what business you may be in, creating emotional bonds is essential to closing deals and maintaining repeat business. We consumers tend to bond with brands that create feelings of fulfillment, belonging, trust, and reciprocity at every touch point of our journey with them. This can be done through personalized communications that is all about the customer, not a generic statement about the brand, events that make customers feel recognized or appreciated, and the like.

For all businesses, creating feelings of belonging and recognition is key for successful customer experiences. One of my favorite social psychologists, Jonathan Haidt, discusses in his book, *The Happiness Hypothesis*, how being part of a tribe contributes to happiness. When we feel like we are part of something that matters, we form friendships with others we deem to be just like us, which creates a sense of belonging with others that understand and support us. This feeling of belonging can result in very strong commitment to the tribe—its members, its rituals, its beliefs. In addition to sparking dopamine through anticipated rewards, religions again, are a great example of creating oxytocin. When we are a part of a religious congregation, we belong to a group of people with like values who become part of our lives in one way or another. Many churches do a great job of creating tribes. Some organize members into congregations of a few hundred people. Within those congregations, members are often assigned volunteer callings to serve one another in some capacity such as a Sunday School teacher, missionary, youth activity organizer. Callings are designed to help keep members of the congregation or "tribe" aligned with the principles of the given church and assure they stay faithful to its principles and rituals. In some cases, adults are assigned to visit other members in their homes as personal ministers sharing gospel lessons and testimonies while checking on their well-being. Interacting with members of your tribe multiple times a week helps to maintain strong bonds with individuals and the organization's belief structure that brought you all together in the first place. And it makes it harder to leave. If you decided you did not believe in your chosen religion anymore, you risk losing respect and friendships if you leave and go find a new church; especially when people around you have invested in you personally.

The tribal nature of religions presents an important concept to business owners. Find a way to bring your customers together to form bonds over your brand, just like church goers form bonds over their common religious beliefs and devotion to service. Invest in your customers in ways that make switching hard to do for what they will be giving up. There are many brands that do a great job of building tribes with similar bonds.

Red Bull produces high energy events to match its popular high energy drinks. They host extreme sports events around the world bringing together athletes and spectators who live out extraordinary experiences amid Red Bull signage and drinks, while making friendships that often last beyond the event itself. These events are hugely popular worldwide and sparked a new product line for the brand, Red Bull TV.

When you bond with others around a cause, experience, product or a brand, your loyalty tends to go up as switching brands or religions if you will, means leaving the tribe, which changes friendships.

Cortisol

Cortisol is most commonly known as the fight or flight hormone. When we experience unusual episodes of stress, we tend to feel a need to either fight to overcome the obstacle or fly away to a safer place. On Wall Street, cortisol has a strong impact on investors. When financial investors sense market volatility, they become increasingly risk adverse. Consumers react the same way. When our jobs or local economies seem unstable, we tend to hunker down and not spend much on unnecessary items and take few risks associated with opportunities that might have pay off potential. As explained by the loss aversion principle referenced earlier, our innate fear of losing what we have becomes elevated when we are surrounded by uncertainty, which elevates our levels of cortisol and risk aversion. This bodes well for products that minimize risk of loss, like insurance, warranties, food storage, power generators, and products associated with survival.

If your business falls into a category associated with avoiding loss, understanding how cortisol drives behavior is key. The higher the stress or fear of loss, the higher the chance of purchasing products and services that prevent that loss. For example, if you offer solutions for protecting against cybersecurity, you would want to emphasize the depth of potential loss in your marketing and create experiences that assure customers you are the one that can protect them from a disaster that could occur by failing to protect customer data or complying with regulatory requirements.

Your customer experiences should help decrease the stress in decision making and create a comfortable, low-risk environment for purchasing items that may not be mainstream to daily routines or needs. A good way to add comfort to the decision process is to offer generous return policies. When we know we can take something back at any time for any reason, we tend to shop more impulsively and likely spend more than usual. Another way to take out perceived risk and create more comfort for purchasing new items is to provide free trials that can be easily cancelled before a charge goes through.

If you are in the B2B space and offering a complex product such as software solutions that require integration with other business systems, chances are your customers are stressed about the choice they need to make as a bad choice could sideline operations, which in turn could have big consequences on their career, job security, and more. Too much stress over potential consequences can lead to indecision and longer decision cycles. Your customer experiences should be built around helping purchasers make informed, wise decisions that minimize the risk of failure and the consequences they fear. Educational events and content such as educational, informative blogs and objective decision guides are key to building a sense of security around your brand.

Finally, a key psychological concept to keep in mind as you build a brand and supporting experiences to attract and maintain your targeted customers is Maslow's hierarchy of needs. Maslow's pyramid of needs starts on a foundation of basic human essentials such as food and shelter, followed by safety, love and belonging needs, and then self-esteem. The apex of Maslow's hierarchy of needs is self-actualization or the achievement of becoming one's highest self having reached lifelong goals such as reaching the top of your game in a profession, sport, or an influencer for social causes.

It may seem many of the behavioral theories cater to minimizing fears of losing status, opportunities, and more. However this does not mean all our marketing needs to talk to our fears. Marketing to aspirations is critical too. Per the luxury market mentioned earlier, people will overspend if they aspire to feel and appear superior in social settings. People will also invest in achieving their aspirations. If your business is to help people self-actualize in sports, business, the arts, writing novels or business books, then map out how you can do this and communicate with the same level of passion they have for their goals. Building marketing and experiences around aspirations and associated emotional fulfillment is a critical cornerstone for differentiation, engagement, sales, and loyalty.

In short, it is important to understand the trends, attitudes, and purchasing criteria that influence your customers, and their influencers. Most consumers assign loyalty to brands that have a value that goes beyond the products and services sold. Knowing what matters to consumers and what may cause them to switch from another brand to your brand is critical to crafting the right messaging and experiences that will enable you to more efficiently grow sales, retain customers, and set your business up for sustainable growth.

GO TIME

Connect Your Brand to Survival DNA.

When mapping out your psychological appeal for your business, first identify what type of survival you offer. Social? Professional? Emotional? Aspirational? When you can align your services and products with what customers need to survive in various aspects of the human journey, you cease to be a vendor and become a valued partner.

Map Out Your ESPs

Start an Excel spreadsheet and title it "ESP Triggers." In this spreadsheet, you will document the elements of choice associated with your business category. You don't need to do your own neuro research to understand the fundamental emotions driving your business. Again, if you are in insurance, people purchase your product primarily from the fear of losing what they have. You provide them with the security of avoiding loss. If you are selling competitive athletic equipment, you are selling the assurance that they have the tools to enable training to pay off so they can reach their performance goals. If you own a restaurant, you are selling a food and/or experience, convenience of not cooking, a place to bond with friends or family, and in some cases, status of dining out in a place that reflects the community to which customers want to belong.

> Column One: Note which emotional elements discussed above are most related to the appeal of your brand: fear of monetary, time, social, or other losses; anticipation of meeting performance, social, or relationship goals; desire to achieve professional advancement and personal wealth, etc.

> Column Two: State how you fulfill the emotional outcomes consumers seek when purchasing in your category. Back to insurance, do you offer policies that guarantee against loss of home, car, business, or income? Do you offer cutting edge tools for ski racers, or proven nutrition supplements for runners that can help them optimize competitive performances and get them closer to their athletic goals? What emotional outcomes do people anticipate from your brand besides the product? Security? Pride? Relief? Confidence? Euphoria?

> Column Three: List the social influencers of brand choices. Do consumers look for social proof, endorsements from authorities, products that are scarce, exclusive, or status oriented? What behavioral economic activities define their purchasing processes. For example, one behaviorial economic activity is mental anchoring which happens when we use an outdated or irrelevant reference to make decisions. We see this in finance when investors just can't get rid of a low performing stock in their portfolio because years ago it was their best return.

What erroneous references, assumptions or myths might exist in your category that throw people off. If you are selling CBD products, you might have to change the notion that cannabis is a questionable entertainment product and educate consumers about the healing effects of CBD's anti-inflammatory and medical nature. Note any rational and irrational influencers of which you are aware.

Column 4: Now go to the websites of your top three to five competitors. Document the elements of choice to which they are appealing. For conscious choices, are they appealing to price? Return on investment? Are they appealing to some of the unconscious triggers we've discussed such as FOMO, the inherent need to self-actualize or excel in a given area, social status? Note how they appeal to survival triggers, scarcity, and so on, and any added values that make them more attractive than others in your category. If their appeals are similar to your own, you will need to find creative ways to differentiate similar claims and promises.

This worksheet is the blueprint for your brand's positioning and messaging strategies. It is a very dynamic document that needs to be updated regularly and monitored to ensure the marketing campaigns and customer experiences you create for your brand align with your ESPs and stand apart from those of your competitors.

CHAPTER 4

Building Customer Experiences for Sales and Loyalty

Few products or services are really unique, or will remain that way for long. You have to offer your target customers something longer lasting; emotionally-fulfilling experiences built on your distinct ESPs. These are brand experiences that go beyond transactions and the functionality of whatever you sell. To do this you need to understand what consciously and unconsciously motivates us humans to assign loyalty to one brand over another.

This chapter covers:

❭ Defining a customer experience that helps you outpace competitors to repeat sales and referrals

❭ Building a brand community

❭ Crafting distinct transactional experiences worth repeating

❭ Elements of a customer experience plan

❭ Building on winning customer experience programs to achieve customer success

When you understand what motivates consumers to act, and the cognition that influences perceptions and biases about brands and products, you can then build highly effective customer experiences. Your customer experience strategy is not just about what you do to make it easy and fulfilling to do business with you, it's how you make each customer feel about your brand during a transaction, before, and after. The key is not to just create good feelings about your brand by being responsive and customer-centric, but also to help your customers feel good, even euphoric, about themselves. When you trigger feelings of self-worth, purpose, status, fulfillment, and even belonging, you will likely spark sales and customer loyalty.

As you build experiences around the principles of behavior economics discussed earlier, you are in a sense creating your brand's ESPs. Few products or services are really unique, or will remain that way for long. You have to offer your target customers something longer lasting: experiences that fulfill your ESPs. These are brand experiences that go beyond transactions and the functionality of whatever you sell.

Your ESPs are what set your brand apart from others. And what will put you on a path to sustainable success as a result. Deciding the kind of ESP experience you want and need to deliver to customers is a critical first step in building a successful marketing plan. All your branding, messaging, touch points, and content need to enhance and support the ESP experience you define and promise to customers.

Keep in mind that customer experience strategies are multi-faceted. You need to define the experience of doing business with you, and the experiences that go beyond the products and services sold, such as those associated with being part of a tribe, a loyalty program, VIP events, membership privileges, community, and so on.

Building Experiences around Community

First, let's start with building a customer experience around community.

A friend of mine, Anne Marie Ohly, has owned one of the leading real estate and property management companies in Colorado's high country for close to 40 years. She started her business in property management, and morphed to real estate sales when her clients trusted no one but her to help them sell the properties she managed. She earned this trust by providing stellar customer service and creating a sense of belonging to a bigger community among her clients. Anne Marie often hosts special events for clients, bringing them together to celebrate living in Colorado's Summit County and make friendships around their mutual connection, Anne Marie. She also emails clients regularly with news about events and happenings around the county that is home to four of Colorado's most popular ski resorts, rivers, and hundreds of hiking trails, keeping them informed of the greater community. Additionally, Anne Marie never stops serving clients, even if they may not represent business opportunities to her ever again. She has a list of home maintenance professionals she shares with each client, and jumps in to make sure clients and service providers connect quickly if there's ever a crisis. She doesn't earn commission from facilitating connections. It's just part of serving the community associated with her brand—buyers and sellers, and home services providers. As a result, she has a long list of loyal partners who quickly refer her to anyone needing property management or help selling or buying a property. This community of buyers, sellers, property managers, and maintenance professionals, all of whom she serves in ways that make them feel recognized and valued, has helped her grow to one of the most successful businesses in her market and maintain sustainable revenue growth.

As you build your business vision, and a supporting marketing plan, pay attention to the community that surrounds you and your business now. How can you expand into supporting communities, e.g., maintenance professionals to refer to home buyers, so that your network of people doing business with you and referring business to you is continuously engaged with your brand and has a steady path to growth.

Being part of a meaningful community is a key reason people stay connected to brands. Brand communities go far beyond physical events that spark conversations online, in person, or expand networking. Online communities are growing rapidly and bring a much bigger pool of people together. Just look at how quickly pages for true crime fanatics pop up and scale to six-digit followers whenever there is a new crime mystery to solve. Same goes for a winning sports team. When a sports team rules their playoff games and wins a championship, thousands of new fans tend to join fan pages on social media to follow their new heroes and bask in conversations about their triumph.

Your online community is a large element of your overall customer experience, and where you can more quickly build and nurture a brand tribe. To succeed, you need to foster a supportive community, monitor the comments and activities, stay engaged with members, and work to keep members engaged with each other while adding overall value for your brand. The larger your online community, the larger your base for marketing outreach, promotions, user/customer surveys, reviews, referrals, and so on. Building a base of followers on social media channels is critical for growth, especially at a time when brand familiarity and credibility often influence sales more than traditional promotions.

Online communities cannot be simply a page where you post product and sales information. Your digital environments must add value and inspire members to post stories, experiences associated with your brand and products, and engage with you and each other. If you are starting a new nutrition bar, you can post a lot of content to get people talking about what they like, don't like, and how your product enhanced an experience for them. Consider:

> ❯ Posting polls about what flavors people like most

> ❯ Sparking discussion by asking members to guess the secret ingredient in your product vs. competitors

> ❯ Hosting a user-generated content contest by inviting members to post stories about favorite places they pulled out and ate your nutrition bar and got a "natural high"? Was it running atop one of Colorado's 14ers, along the beach in Torrey Pines, sailing among the islands surrounding Portland, Maine, or during a personal best golf event? Make it even more engaging by asking members to vote for their favorite stories.

> ❯ Posting industry research on nutrition and related topics that support healthy activities and power surges via the right nutritional fix

There is really no end to the content you can create and post to your online community.

Elevating Transactional Customer Experiences

One of the most talked about aspects of customer experience is the process you set up for people to do business with you. Today's consumers have little to zero tolerance for companies that don't respond quickly to inquiries or customer service needs. And with the entire world being at our fingertips via online commerce, we can easily and quickly switch to a brand that meets our expectations for how we believe we should be treated in exchange for our business and ultimately loyalty. We consumers want to set the rules for brand relationships, return policies, and how we do business. We want options for browsing businesses' offerings, purchasing online, in-store, or purchasing online and picking up in person. If we can't find a website to browse products for a retailer we see when driving around town, we often won't consider going there in person to shop. We are picky because we can be.

As an entrepreneur you need to provide as many options as possible for how people can do business with you and make it as easy as possible at the same time. And as an entrepreneur just getting started, you will likely have limited resources, making it hard to be everything to everyone. So to start, identify the top priorities among your core customer targets and put most of your initial efforts into meeting these needs, expanding into innovative new ways to serve existing and niche groups as revenue allows.

To determine the top focus for your customer experience, ask yourself what you want your customers to say about you. Do you want them to tell others:

❯ About your extraordinary product quality

❯ About the convenience of doing business with you online and offline

❯ How they got great value for the price they paid

❯ How you and your staff made them feel like they were your most important customer

❯ What it felt like to do business with you—was it fun? Inspiring? Gratifying?

People talk about the things they experienced with a brand that were memorable and meaningful to them so be sure to give them something to talk about.

What is the value you want people to think of when they see your logo, store front, or get your marketing messages?

> ❱ Do you want to be seen as a partner that supports clients beyond the products sold, offering advice or insights that help them enhance their own profitability?

> ❱ Do you want to be known for responsiveness and customer service? For exceeding expectations and raising the bar for you and your competitors?

> ❱ Do you want people to feel they got good value for the price paid due to offering offerings or bundled packages others might not?

Shopify listed some of the experiences customers expect in 2023 and will likely continue to expect for years to come. These include:

> ❱ Payment options and safety in online transactions. To meet this expectation, accept multiple credit cards, not just the one you get the best rate with, so that customers have a choice. Make sure they know you comply with cybersecurity best practices and regulations so they can count on safe and secure transactions.

> ❱ On this same note, let customers shop your online stores from the channels they use the most. Social channels, even TikTok, are increasingly offering sales transactions that align with engaging content. Don't skip the opportunity to create a sales experience in a setting your customers already use and trust.

> ❱ When possible, let customers do business with you offline and online. Many shoppers want to experience a product or brand in person, but ultimately place their orders online. Customers wanting to see your store, your office, meet your people, to get a "feel" for how you operate should have that option if it's something you can affordably provide.

> ❱ Studies show shopping via a smartphone is growing at a steady rate. So, if you are in retail, make sure your website is responsive and allows a seamless experience for mobile users.

⟩ Personalization is key. With simple CRM tools you can personalize emails, promotions, live chats, and other direct consumer communications specific to each customer's relationship with you. This is not just a nice thing to do, it's expected. Many reports show customers will switch brands if a given one is not willing to personalize experiences around their historical transactions or expressed needs. Various studies show the majority of consumers are willing to give brands personal information if it will be used to elevate personalization.

⟩ Sustainability is not a passing fad just as personalization was not. More than 70 percent of consumers state that doing business with brands that focus on sustainability in production and operations is somewhat to very important to them. As Gen Z, the generation of consumers age 12–27 in 2024 who are known for being concerned about climate change, continues to have more shopping power, expect this to be even more important across B2B and B2C sales. Promote your sustainability commitments in your marketing and throughout your customer experience.

Elements of a Winning Customer Experience Plan

There are many great examples of customer experiences for both in-person and online shopping. Some are quite complex like retail stores offering personal shoppers, booking events of various types at their locations, and providing travel services to help customers get there. Others using Augmented Reality (AR) and Artificial Intelligence (AI) to let people experience products in real time at home, on their phones, in-store, wherever they want to be. And others that go the extra mile to make life easier for customers. As AI and AR continue to change the way we live, new customer experiences will manifest and so too will the expectations among customers for those new experiences.

A great example of customer experience utilizing new technology is the many apps that let you "try on" make up or hair color virtually which is a lot easier than in person. One example of a brand doing this is L'Oréal, which offers an augmented reality experience through a platform called Modiface. You can go to loreal.com and click on the app and virtually try on new hair colors and make up and see your look transform live in real time. When you can instantly "experience" what you look like with pink hair, fire-engine red lipstick, or a darker shade of foundation, the risk of dissatisfaction is lower and you are likely to purchase something new or different. Having those options from one brand and not another just might make you more likely to go back to that brand instead of vet out other options down the road.

DoorDash presents a good example of building on a business model you have already mastered. This leader in home delivery expanded its stronghold in its industry by adding other conveniences such as grocery pick up, retail store pick up, and even package pick up from the post office or other mail delivery franchises. They've taken the value of their service—convenience—to a new level and created a membership program to make it more affordable and valuable. DoorDash memberships cost a small monthly fee and provides free delivery, credit back if you pick up an order yourself, and discounts on deliveries not provided for free. No commitment or contract requirement makes this an even greater convenience.

While searching Google for the best coffee shop in Grand Junction, Colorado, I found Colorado Craft Coffee and Beer House with a 5-star average for 167 reviews, most of which were more about the experience than the craft products sold. So I stopped by. I quickly noticed a large bookshelf filled with games that come in a box instead of on your phone and then signs promoting Tuesday Beer Bingo and Friday Couples' Trivia. I asked the owner, James Ferguson, who was called out for his friendliness in many reviews, why he had so many 5.0 reviews on Google. Did he roast his own coffee, brew his own beer? His answer was a quick no. He explained his business was not about having the best coffee and beer in town, but about selling locals a chance to experience coffee and beer crafted throughout Colorado in a place that fostered community and fun. He vets brews from popular towns like Boulder, Breckenridge, Telluride, and offers them for a few days before switching them out for others, assuring customers a new experience every visit.

Added to the experience is how he treats people like old friends. I ordered the latte special, he applied a discount and refused a tip, asking me to come back instead. It seems to be working as 70% of his business is repeat and his revenue stream keeps growing.

This story about Colorado Craft Coffee and Beer House highlights the importance of experiences delivered as equal to if not greater than products offered. James does not offer unique products like other coffee shops and breweries that craft their own formulas, and he does not offer food other than simple snacks also sourced from Colorado businesses. Just a distinct experience to try Colorado's best craft brews and enjoy a gathering place to mingle, meet new people, and have fun. Finding a way to add a new twist to an old experience can set businesses in many industries apart.

Oh, that Irish Cream Latte I ordered? Best ever! Other coffee shops will be hard pressed to beat it.

On the B2B side of business, American Express offers a product for small businesses called BluePrint. It is essentially a dashboard that helps you easily track expenses, account balances, payments, and other personal aspects of your business's finances. The experience offered is far more than a friendly and timely service for issues regarding your American Express accounts. Blueprint offers the ability to link accounts from other financial and banking institutions to your dashboard, making the service truly about the customer, not the brand. You can also apply for a loan and hear back faster than most other channels, and when approved, the funds go right into your BluePrint account, making it simple and convenient. Going a step further, Blueprint sets you up to take credit card transactions from all major card brands—Visa, Mastercard, and Discover—letting you use competitive cards on the American Express system and allowing you to give your customers options, which keeps them happy and coming back to your business. This is a game-changing example of a customer-centric experience as American Express is offering something that is designed to be what the customer really needs, not what they need to keep you committed to them in ways that may not be in your best interest.

As a startup, in any industry, both B2C and B2B, you can stand out among established brands with similar experiences:

≫ Consider hosting events in your store or online that enable customers to experience how your products and brands can directly enhance their lives. Maybe you can't afford to provide an AR tool that creates instant product experiences but you can set up a free session for personal shopping, makeup tutorials, and the like.

▶ Personal shoppers are not just for retail and fashion stores. Make it easy and obligation free for your prospects to schedule time with you and your team members to ask questions and compare your products to alternatives. In the process, you might just form a personal relationship that will matter more than the price you quote vs. a competitor.

▶ Have a cool building or workspace? Offer to rent it out for company retreats. Maybe offer to set up technology demos for people wanting to know about the development of your product or services. One of my favorite experiences was working for a manufacturing robotics company. Robots all over the plant floor were programmed to do some amazing things on assembly lines. When we went to trade shows, these robots could be programmed to take and hand out business cards, serve swag, or even serve drinks. Imagine what you can do to demonstrate your products in unexpected ways.

▶ How can you create a Members Only experience around your brand? This concept has worked well for American Express which has lived by its "Membership Has Its Privileges" mantra for decades, and for new companies like DoorDash. Imagine new ways you can make your customers' lives easier that are worth paying for, either by the project or a monthly subscription.

Take note of interesting, extraordinary, and interactive experiences brands in your category, and others, offer. How can you replicate the ones that are getting customers to come back for more and refer others? Executing customer experiences at the community and personal level is critical to getting your startup off the ground, and for building the kind of customer base for sustainable sales.

Keep in mind, setting protocols for customer interaction for all your team members is essential, and choosing to work with partners and ancillary companies that reflect your same values and service is key. You will always be judged by the company you keep in this customer-driven world.

Customer Success is the Ultimate Customer Experience

The experience with your brand does not stop with the sales contract or when the product arrives. It goes well beyond the transaction to assure each customer has a highly productive and satisfying experience. This is where Customer Success needs to be an integral part of your overall customer experience plan.

Customer success is driven by the processes you put in place to assure each customer optimizes potential outcomes from using your product. You should not just be focused on helping customers like their experience with your brand transactions and customer service. You should also be focused on helping them achieve the goals, personal or professional, around which they purchased your product. This is the foundation of loyalty, lifetime value, and referrals.

To help customers have successful experiences, your marketing plan needs to include some basic elements such as setting up online shopping channels, in-store browsing experiences, and make it easy to shop from the device or channel customers prefer. Other considerations include:

Satisfaction Outreach: After transactions, send an email to assess satisfaction with each aspect of their experience with you, and ask for suggestions to do better. Including a Net Promoter Score (NPS) survey gives customers a quick and consistent way to provide feedback. Essentially, your NPS score shows the likelihood your customers will refer others to you, and truthfully, that says it all. Per the social aspects of referring a brand to others, this is a strong metric of potential repeat sales and loyalty.

Generous Return Policies: As mentioned before, you want to spark trial for your products and your brand by taking the fear out of the shopping experience. Let customers make returns for any reason. Enabling people to change their mind without punishment makes it easier to get people to try something new for the first time.

Customer success starts and continues throughout a customers' lifetime of using your products or services. This is especially critical in technology sales whether for business or personal use. Customers will likely need support setting up a new product, integrating new software into their existing technology stacks, switching from one platform to another, and maintaining productivity over time. Setting them up for success is a critical element of brand experience, and something you need to have planned out before you start processing orders.

Many weight loss programs provide solid customer success programs. Instead of just handing over the rationed food, dietary guidelines, and exercise diagrams, many successful programs assign mentors to meet with customers to discuss progress, provide encouragement, and provide tips specific to the challenges of each customer. This way, they deliver not just experiences but more successful outcomes than before, as they have a better chance of keeping people on the plan.

Jan Young, a seasoned customer success expert and consultant, defines customer success as the intersection of customer needs and company objectives. How do you execute successfully on both? You have to first look at how customers want to do business with you, not just what they want in your product. The how is critical to keeping customers buying and referring others to you. You then need to align those needs with how you operate.

Some examples of how customer wants and business needs can align follow:

> ❭ Make it easy to opt out of your communications and your product sales. Many companies trap customers with subscriptions for hard goods that do not need a subscription, like cleaning supplies that you are not likely to go through quickly. Multilevel marketing companies are prime contributors to this trap as many require distributors or resellers to order inventory monthly whether they need it or not. This is counter to customer centricity which is based on the simple premise of letting customers buy when they want and need to, not due to a requirement of monthly purchases for products not yet needed.

> ❭ Make it easy to use your product with other brands. Apple takes choices away and forces their price points and profit goals on you by making computers that can only use Apple charging cords, sync with only Apple watches, and so on. No integration means no choices and no savings for customers.

❯ When someone wants out of a brand relationship, let them go gracefully. Suing customers for wanting out of long-term contracts when you let them down, or their business profits changed due to a pandemic or other unforeseeable events, burns bridges and reputations as you can count on them telling others about their disappointing experience.

❯ Keep relationships alive. Create a segment in your CRM database for lost customers and reach out with educational, soft-sell messages every once in a while. Let them know where you've improved or grown since you parted ways. Be sure to include companies you lost to another provider during a sales pitch as you could set yourself up for another chance to win their business.

❯ Customer success is rooted in freedom and flexibility. Give them freedom to buy on their terms, not a forced subscription or contract that lasts longer than your business might last, and the flexibility to use other brands with your products to save them time and money.

GO TIME

Back to your Excel spreadsheet file. Now create a worksheet in the same file as the one you started in Chapter 3 and title it "Community." Here is where you will document the kind of community, engagement, brand experiences, which your customers are likely to want to be a part of.

If you market directly to consumers, go to Facebook, Instagram, and X (formerly Twitter), and start browsing pages of brands you admire in your category. Note the content they post that engages target customers, any content generated by users, and what followers of the brand are posting in comments. Note which topics get the most likes, shares or reposts from members of that brand page or online community. If you are in B2B, go to LinkedIn and look up the pages of your top competitors. Document the topics they post about that get the most responses and likes from their followers, and what type of feedback they get in the comments.

Map out activities and marketing assets you can execute for an online community. Podcasts and webinars, and online resources pages of items like glossaries, industry trends reports, and case studies are examples of elements that successfully engage online communities. Do the same for your offline communities, which may include those built by live demo events, trade shows, community fairs, and so on. Note the experiences offered by your competitors and take note of how those experiences compete with the ones you plan to develop. Then go do better. Outline how you plan to serve customers, set them up for successful on boarding, provide support for customer success, and how you will handle cancellations, returns, and other events that can impact your reputation.

PART 2

BUILDING AND EXECUTING A MARKETING PLAN

A costly mistake entrepreneurs make is to do something just because they can. Another is starting something new and not sticking with it. To use resources wisely, stay on track, and grow your business, you need a plan and process to stay with it.

This section will outline the key elements of a marketing plan, actions that need to be part of your weekly routine, and tools that can help you automate execution and monitor results. You'll learn how to set up SEO, CRM, Google Ads, personalized email campaigns, and more, in addition to establishing thought leadership in your field which is key to building networks and credibility that build sales.

CHAPTER 5

Mapping Out a Plan and a Process You Can Stick With

This chapter will review key elements of marketing strategy and actionables to help you achieve your marketing and revenue goals. It will help you lay out a plan that you can execute consistently and affordably. You will gain insights about how to:

> ❯ Stake out your position and purpose

> ❯ Price for the distinct values you offer

> ❯ Set promotions up to pay off

> ❯ Plan to distribute your product

> ❯ Effectively and efficiently execute your marketing

> ❯ Budget for any budget

> ❯ Set and monitor metrics

The Merriam-Webster dictionary defines "plan" as a noun as: *an orderly arrangement of parts of an overall design or objective;*

❯ *a method for achieving an end*

❯ *an often customary method of doing something: Procedure*

❯ *a detailed formulation of a program of action*

The above is precisely how every entrepreneur needs to look at marketing. It's a plan of action, not a document to be filed away; a process, not just something you do when you have time or feel creative. It's a detailed roadmap for how you will achieve key business goals such as brand awareness, lead generation, and conversion. You map out the steps you need to take, the parts you need to arrange, and the tools you need to successfully execute actions against your objective. And then you put in place the daily routines and processes to complete the journey. On time and on budget.

When building a business, having a comprehensive plan that outlines action items, due dates, and metrics against revenue goals is critical to success. Executing all the elements consistently vs. sporadically is often the difference between success and failure. You can't get far in a car with no fuel or battery power, just like you can't catch up with established brands if you don't keep your foot on the pedal for brand awareness, consumer engagement, lead generation, and conversion.

Elements of an Actionable and Affordable Marketing Plan

Following are key elements of an actionable and affordable marketing plan. Add these elements to the Excel spread sheet you are creating to document and notate who you are, where you are going, and what you intend to achieve. Keep in mind plans change, as they should change as nothing is static in business, or any aspect of life for that matter. Your markets, customers, and competitions will change as will your own goals, realities, offerings, and tactics to succeed. This is meant to be a fluid document you refer to and update regularly. It is your guide, and voice of reason to keep you on the path to success despite the many distractions that will come your way.

Stake Out Your Market Position and Purpose

Your positioning strategy is critical as it defines your value to your core customers and the market in general. You need to find your place in your world and put a stake in the ground. Trying to be everything to everyone does not work. You are not selling yourself short to market to a small defined customer population. You are setting yourself up for sustainable success, which you can build on to expand your market pool as your revenues and capital grow.

Starting up, identify a market position you can ultimately own in the markets in which you operate, or at least do well in as you build your base. Is that position the price leader for entry-level or cost-conscious consumers in your space? Is that position a customer service leader in a space dominated by brands more focused on sales than service? Are you hoping to set new fashion, cosmetic, lifestyle or home décor trends? Or offer ways for businesses to do old things better?

In short, answer this question as best you can now: What segment of your defined consumer universe are you set up to serve today and what segments do you intend to serve as you grow?

Once you answer the above, you need to gather as much insight on this segment as possible so you can have meaningful conversations via your communications and marketing channels. These insights include purchase criteria, decision processes, emotional and tangible influencers, price tolerance/intolerance, purchase intent, frequency, and transactional value. No short exercise, but one that is mission critical and needed often as your customers and their influencers and triggers change rapidly and frequently. Especially in trendy categories like fashion and lifestyle.

As discussed earlier, a big part of a brand's position is its purpose. Your purpose is a subset of your market position and needs to have similar relevance. If your product is built around a movement, like providing shoes for children in underprivileged communities around the world like that of TOMS, or raising funds to eradicate poverty, include positioning statements or slogans that reflect your position and purpose. Cotopaxi's slogan, *Gear for Good,* presents an innuendo that reflects the value it offers consumers via good gear for good times, and the value it offers society by donating to good causes worldwide.

Aligning with a purpose that is related to your product category will help consumers more quickly associate your brand with your values, and theirs. If you offer software to help bookstores better manage their business, perhaps your purpose is to help give indie writers a voice by hosting a new distribution channel for books that don't fit big publishers' criteria for quick sales. If your product is in the fashion industry, can you find a way to support students in fashion design so they can unleash their creativity through design vs. manage retail stores selling others' work? Once you define your purpose you need to define how you will communicate it in your promotional endeavors.

Your positioning will inform the development of your ESPs and the messaging that helps your brand speak to the minds and souls of your target customers.

Pricing for the Distinct Values You Offer

As discussed in Chapter 1, a brand's values are multi-faceted:

> ❯ Product quality value

> ❯ Price to value ratio

> ❯ Social position

> ❯ CSR—corporate social responsibility

> ❯ ESG—environmental, social, and governance

Your plan needs to define how you can live these values now as you get started with minimal resources, and how you intend to evolve in living these values larger as you grow. We've discussed the social, CSR, and ESG values earlier, and if you're doing the homework, you've started notating these values in your plan.

Here you need to document your plans for pricing and the price to value ratio you want to establish in order to appeal to the customers you seek most. Research shows, including much of the inspiring work done by Daniel Ariely, professor of psychology and behavioral economics at Duke University and author of *Predictably Irrational,* we consumers tend to gravitate toward the middle. If you give us a menu that shows your best entrée priced at $50, and your least impressive one at $15, and a few options in the middle around $25, we will order one around the midpoint of the price range as the middle feels safe to us. The high end might be a splurge we can't always afford, the low end might be seen as not worthy of where we see ourselves socially, or where we want to be. As a new brand, starting out as the splurge option could negatively impact sales as your distinctiveness might not be known to target consumers yet. If you are banking on revenue from sales to fund growth, this approach could cement you to the slow track.

As discussed earlier, you cannot price a new product as a luxury item if your brand is not perceived to be luxury and worth the premium price. But you can price it somewhere between the low and high end of your market pricing thresholds. You do not want to be the low-cost leader unless you are a commodity and must compete on bulk sales. Pricing somewhere in the middle positions your brand as worth more than a commodity but affordable for consumers to try.

Consider the following pricing approaches to help you enter the market and stake out the position you seek.

》 Set a GTM (Go-to-Market) price to spark trial as you launch. The goal is to get as many people as possible to try your brand, get hooked, and refer others. It needs to be priced right to minimize the risk for consumers buying something they have not experienced yet in order to know if it lives up to its claims for value and function. Be careful not to discount your introductory price to the point that you establish yourself in the budget bracket. If your goal is to be in the mid-market tier of your category, set your launch price slightly lower than those with whom you want to compete in terms of position and appeal.

》 Communicate the value for the price you charge. Define the ESP for your product and build your key messages and brand persona accordingly. Are your products designed to give the owners a new sense of style, enhanced job performance, better athletic outcomes? Are they designed to be more functional than fashionable to help simplify daily routines? Your messaging, brand iconology, and product imagery need to reflect the value and social status you believe will appeal to your core target customers and the corresponding conscious and unconscious triggers of choice.

❯ Once you define the values you want to project, you need to assure target consumers that your product holds up to your promises, and the expectation they have of getting value for the price. As you add more features to new product releases, you can more justifiably increase your price.

❯ Create a higher end version of your product as you are able. But keep the old product at or near its original price to help you draw practical, and even aspirational customers to your brand. Use your higher priced products to help you increase revenue and profits while you keep marketing to the greater masses that can sustain you with volume. Do something distinctive to justify moving toward luxury pricing if that is your goal.

A tiered pricing approach can work well across categories for both B2C and B2B. For example, SaaS companies might launch with an initial release that serves a specific need within a given category. They can keep that basic product available to draw customers to their brand while enhancing the second release with new features, customer service packages, and more to justify a higher price point, longer contractual agreement, and investment in the brand as a long-term partner. In many cases, your first product release is how you can attract customers whom you can ultimately convert to higher level customers over time, or just keep happy for repeat sales to help you fund new releases.

Setting Promotions Up to Pay Off

Marketing is the most fun aspect of business, far more than arranging numbers, in my humble opinion, and promotion is the foundation of why. This is where imagination, innovation, and invention come to play. Without limit. It's also one of the most challenging, not because it's expensive or void of channels, but because consumers are more inundated with marketing stimuli than the human mind can keep up with. Due to the ongoing instant gratification many consumers experience from immediate responses from digital apps constantly used on computers and smart phones, and access to fast-paced information channels, the average attention span continues to fall. According to Dr. Gloria Mark, author of *Attention Span: A Groundbreaking Way to Restore Balance, Happiness and Productivity* our attention span is around 47 seconds when viewing a screen. But in general, we humans have an attention span shorter than that of a goldfish, 8.25 seconds vs. 9 seconds, according to data reported by bridgecareaba.com. With so many brands trying to get the attention of the same consumers you are, it's getting harder to engage consumers with ads of any kind—digital, print, outdoor, social, etc. No one really knows the actual number of ads we see a day, but we all know it's far too many now that we get ads on apps we use daily on our computers and phones, Facebook, LinkedIn, YouTube, Instagram, TikTok, and the games we play when social channels fail to keep our attention.

Before you can effectively execute promotional plans that drive sales, you need to focus on promoting the awareness of your brand among the consumer groups you target. With all the ads that one can click on any given channel, consumers are more likely to click on the ones for familiar brands more than those they have never heard of before. Creating a multi-faceted promotional plan that creates awareness while inspiring consumers to engage with your brand is a cornerstone for all marketing success. Some of the elements of promotion you need to execute to achieve acquisition and retention goals include:

⟩ **Awareness / Familiarity**—The 45th president of the United States largely won because voters had heard of him. Many voters did not know much about his qualifications to govern the country, or position on key national and world issues, but just knowing his name was enough to earn their votes. This behavior is aligned with the mere-exposure effect, also known as the familiarity principle. The power of familiarity is why a first-time presidential candidate became the unlikely winner. He knew any headline, good, bad, and ugly, is a good headline as it creates familiarity and familiarity wins political campaigns, consumer attention, sales and loyalty. People won't remember what they heard about you in many cases, but quite often they will remember your name.

Achieving awareness for a new brand is much more affordable than in the past as you can reach mass audiences with organic and low-cost efforts on multiple digital channels. Many let you decide what you want to pay for a designated number of brand impressions vs. tell you what you owe. Your metric for awareness marketing is exposure. How many people can you expose your brand to at the lowest cost possible? Outlining actions toward this goal is a key part of your promotional plan. As you map plans to gain awareness, consider all the channels on which your targets spend time, and note the topics that get the most impressions, likes, and shares. Your plan needs to include concerted and regular actions to insert your brand into these stories with responses to posts on hot topics and related original content on your own pages. While it's good to get exposure through impressions to your ad, keep in mind that impressions do not equal leads. But maintaining good levels of impressions can help set your ads up for higher success via the familiarity principle mentioned earlier.

❯ **Communications**—Your communications plan needs to be multi-faceted. It's not just about communications designed to sell products and services anymore. It's about communications designed to protect and build brand reputations and build relationships that spark trial, loyalty, lifetime value, and referrals. The primary elements of your marketing plan need to include content that educates targets and enables them to make their own informed decisions while positioning your brand as an authority in your space.

Your communications plan should outline:

- Content you can develop to establish brand leadership and engage customers with informative, educational insights that help them make wise decisions.
- Tools in which you will need to invest so that you can deliver highly personalized communications to leads in your sales funnel, and customers in your revenue stream. What email platforms and CRM systems can you afford now, and what features do they have that will grow with you vs. require switching as your marketing needs expand?
- Plans for how you will communicate with thought leaders, influencers, and media in your space to secure highly credible

earned media. In what areas of your space are you an SME (a subject matter expert)? And what stories can you develop around your specific expertise?

- Methods for communicating to all constituent groups to mitigate a crisis or situation that could hurt your brand reputation.

≫ **Thought Leadership**—Leading, or at least contributing to the narrative for your business category is the most credible form of promotion. Primarily because you are not pitching a sale, but sharing expertise that is meaningful for others in your industry. Thought leadership marketing includes securing interviews, feature stories, or guest columns with industry media and influencers that cover your category; presenting at conferences, on webinars; appearing on or hosting podcasts, and the like. Your thought leadership plan should outline the media and influencers, podcast hosts, social media posters, and the like that have an audience you need to reach, and the stories you can offer to each of those entities. Social media such as LinkedIn and Facebook offer strong platforms to build thought leadership as well. Mentions and articles you secure with media outlets is considered "earned media" which sets up your paid media—ads—to pay off more due to familiarity with a brand and the expertise of the given leadership.

Research You Can Afford

A quote from ancient religious leader, Abu Bakr, sums up the importance of ongoing market research: "Without knowledge action is useless and knowledge without action is futile."

As an entrepreneur, you need to keep pace with your target customers' changing mindsets and needs, and how your existing customers feel about doing business with you. It might seem overwhelming, but it does not have to be. Signing up for reports and insights from the global consulting firms outlined in Chapter 2 is a good start, but you need to also gather information directly from your customers. There are many ways you can continually ask your customers what matters to them, much of which can and should be part of your ongoing plan. Research methods can include one-question surveys on your website and your LinkedIn page, requests for rating your service experience at the end of a transaction, follow-up emails asking for reviews of your product, and when applicable, bi-annual client audits to assess what you are doing right and where you can improve.

There are many free to low-cost tools and methods to help you stay on top of customers' perceptions and expectations of your category and brand. Here's a few examples of different formats. I am not providing a long list of brands to explore as by the time this is printed, many will have merged, and others will not exist. Marketing technology changes that quickly and so do the providers.

SurveyMonkey—This is a platform that offers a simple and easy way to create your own surveys and email them directly to your own database. It offers pre-written surveys you can customize and tools to create your own. You can use for free or pay a monthly subscription for more features and products. This is a simple tool that provides questions you can use, helps you craft your own questions in ways to get valid responses, and sorts and graphs the data to help you make sense of what you collected. It's a powerful tool available at affordable prices.

Pollfish—This is a great AI tool that helps you reach global consumer networks in just a few seconds. You type in what you want to learn, e.g., how likely are you to purchase digital home security systems in the next six months? Pollfish's AI tool creates a short survey which you can edit, and their system allows you to send it to their network or your own database. If you use their network, you can sort for demographics like location, language, age, gender, marital status, and more. Their AI shows you the estimated time to get responses, one day in many cases, how many responses you need for validity, and your fee based upon the needed responses.

Research Panels—There are many third-party research panels you can tap to survey people that fit your target population. Research firms organize panels of people who are willing to take surveys about given categories or topics, and then submit your questions to these highly vetted panels for a nominal fee. You can also create your own panel, which typically takes more time and money. A leader in this industry is Qualtrics, but there are many options with many price points to explore.

A note of caution: Consumers are survey weary. Getting even your best customers to take surveys is often a difficult task. With that attention span of 8.25 seconds, which I personally think is a generous statistic, you have to compete for attention more than ever before. The best way to get ongoing information quickly and for free is to do frequent one-question surveys on your website, social pages, and the like. CRM systems like HubSpot often offer free and simple survey tools to send as emails. No matter the tool, the best way to get a response is to keep it simple. And short. And infrequent.

Another important note about surveys: whether you are building your survey tool with AI or writing out the questions yourself, ask only questions that provide the insights you actually need to act on to better serve the needs of your audiences. Don't ask personal or prying questions. Do you really need to know income, marital status, or pronouns? If you are trying to find out what software features you should develop in your next release, keep your questions focused on the outcomes or resources customers need to do whatever they do faster and better.

Distribution Options

Assuming you already have your product in development before reading this book, you likely have some idea for how you plan to distribute your product to your customers. If not, there's no time like now to get started. Distribution strategies clearly vary from category to category, and from B2B and B2C. Here's a few approaches to consider for your distribution plan for both B2B and B2C.

> **Direct:** You can sell products directly to your customers in either the business or consumer space via multiple channels, online and offline such as physical stores, e-commerce sites, and online store fronts on third-party sites like Amazon, eBay, and Etsy. The advantage of selling directly is that you're not giving control of your products' pricing, display, and promotion to intermediaries or resellers, and can keep prices lower in many cases as you're not paying expensive middleman fees.

Building your own e-commerce site keeps your selling prices lower, gives you more control over shopping cart strategies, and does not pit your product against competitors on the same selling site. There are numerous website builders that offer e-commerce functions and shopping cart support and are easy to use. Look at Wix, GoDaddy, Shopify, and Squarespace. However, it takes a lot of time and money to build traffic to your site to get the kind of revenue you need to scale quickly. For this reason, it is smart to use third-party selling sites as well as your own to assure greater exposure to consumers in the act of shopping.

Each third-party selling site has different fee models and opportunities. For one, Amazon operates like a retail store and caters to the buyer experience, while eBay serves as an auction house, or online garage sale, and caters to the seller's needs. Either way, you set up your storefront, list your pricing, and manage the keywords for your products to assure you show up in searches among shoppers on these sites. Each site charges fees for selling on their pages, which are nominal. Amazon and eBay cater to different buyer experiences as well. Amazon is a store front with many options and price points. eBay allows buyers to bid on products and see when pricing will change if they want to hold out for the chance of a lower price.

When choosing direct channels, the most important decision factor is choosing channels your customers use. Whatever fees you spend to sell on Amazon or eBay or the like will quickly be miniscule per the volume you are likely to gain by using these channels over one you have to build, drive customers to, and manage solely by yourself. Keep in mind that the storefronts you build on third-party sites need to be updated regularly, keywords monitored, and more. You need to treat these sites like you do your SEO efforts—continually monitor keywords, search queries, results, impressions, and such.

Indirect: This method covers working with intermediaries like retailers, resellers, and wholesalers that either buy your product outright and then promote, merchandise, and sell directly to consumers. If you sell athleisure, Target or Macy's might be the retailers for you, and distributors specializing in athletic wear or fashion merchandise might be good options for you. If you are in B2B, you will likely grow faster if you form partnerships with companies offering complementary products and cross-sell each others' products. When you do this, you grow your sales team quickly without having to hire people or pay salaries, just the commissions you negotiate upfront.

Intensive: Real quick, this method means that you are putting your products out on as many channels as you can. Retailers' online sites and in-store shelves, multiple e-commerce sites, your own online stores, and so on. The world is your oyster here.

Selective: The opposite of intensive distribution, this is the approach you take when you want to create a sense of exclusivity for your products so you can charge more. Going back to the luxury discussion, where you sell your goods helps to define the perceived value of your brand. Note you will not see Chanel or Versace at JCPenney. If you have a distinct product for a distinguished audience, your products need to be sold in places that are worthy of the reputation and price you seek to sustain over time. If you operate in a niche market, you need to identify niche market distribution points. You can work with a distribution intermediary specializing in niche markets to get your brand in places that already attract your target groups. Be prepared to compete with a lot of other products to get represented by the distributors that serve the outlets you seek to be in. This is where product distinction and quality can make or break a new brand.

Effective, Efficient Execution

You need a plan for how you will execute all the marketing aspects of starting or managing a business. Yes, I know all the things discussed so far seem like more than an entrepreneur can handle, but this is where planning comes in. You need to work in phases. And you need to create a guide that keeps you focused on tasks as they need to be done. Having a good plan in place will also help you identify resources to help you get started and maintain a consistent marketing presence.

Much of the marketing technology available now enables you to work faster and more automated than before. AI can help you come up with written and video content you can edit to reflect your key messages, which consumes less time than starting from scratch. You can also create email copy and automate its delivery to diverse groups at select times. In just seconds, you can separate your cold leads from warm leads, and warm leads from hot leads in closing patterns and communicate with mass personalization per each relationship in play. It just takes setting up systems and staying organized enough to maintain them.

When building out your marketing plan, you should identify the tools you can afford to use for your website, e-commerce stores, CRM/email, customer surveys, and direct marketing. In many cases one subscription with a technology provider will cover multiple needs, allowing you to manage fewer systems and save money. For example, many DIY website platforms offer tools for e-commerce, SEO, and more.

You need to also plan your resources around the decision process for your category. Do you offer a service that requires a sales call, a demo? If this is the case, is live chat generating the kind of volume you need to thrive? Or do you need to engage a call center to follow up quickly, offer relevant conversations per your guidance to keep interested leads warm and move them to a closing pattern? You can pay call centers with expertise in your category in a variety of ways: by the hour, by the minute, or per performance. Some averages as of this writing are:

> By the hour: $25 an hour in the U.S. By the minute: Many call centers tier their by-minute pricing by volume, lowering the cost for more minutes spent. In general, a good budget would be $1 per minute to start.

> Pay per Call: $3–$7 or higher depending on specific needs and categories.

When looking for a call center to follow up with the leads you pay to generate with your digital and other types of marketing ads, take the time to do in-depth research. Remember call centers record their calls for training and accountability. So, you should ask for sample recordings to see how they really engage with clients' leads just like you should ask to talk to current clients to see how they deliver on goals.

In Chapter 12, you will learn more about resource options to optimize the projects you need to execute. How to find and vet freelancers for website maintenance, SEO management, social media production and publishing, cybersecurity, and so much more. For now, just know you can find the help you need to set up marketing systems that work continuously while you spend your time working on innovative new product ideas, finding new partners, pitching funders, prepping for accelerators, meeting with distribution channel managers, and all the other things you need to do to get your business ready to soar.

It goes without saying that you need to be pretty well organized to manage all the aspects of a marketing plan and keep them going. Setting something up and then not regularly monitoring and maintaining it results in wasted time and money you can't get back. Subscribe to a project management software service like Asana or Monday to help you schedule tasks, manage deadlines, adapt as necessary, send reminders and alerts, and monitor impact toward goal. Many project management software tools offer a free entry level pricing tier to help you test them out before committing to paid subscriptions which are typically nominal, like $30 or less per seat per month.

Budgeting for Any Budget

Most startups can't really go by the playbook of setting a marketing budget between 6–10 percent of revenue as most don't start out with any revenue. But if you know how to start a business as outlined in Entrepreneur's book, *Start Your Own Business*, you have already crafted projections around the industry trends and consumer data you reviewed when you read Chapter 2 of this book. A good benchmark for young companies is to spend between 10–20 percent of the overall budget on marketing programs. The more you spend on your GTM launch, the faster you can gain brand awareness and fill up your sales funnel. If you are more established and have traction in your market already, a good range to spend is 5–10 percent of your gross or projected revenue.

Regardless of what you decide to spend, you have to keep in mind the old adage: *to make money, you need to spend money.* If you don't spend enough to reach the people you need to purchase your products, then you have to ask yourself why you are doing what you are doing. Get funding through crowdsourcing, talk to private equity and venture capital firms, work with your bankers. For in-depth guidance on how to fund your business, refer to Entrepreneur's book, *Fund Your Business* which outlines strategies, tips, and tactics for getting the revenue you need to set yourself up for a fast and successful start.

Once you have the money you need, plan how to spend it wisely and manage your budget. You can download some great free budget management templates by HubSpot and other marketing software companies to help you get started. Examples of items you need to budget for to get you started include:

❯ CRM system like HubSpot or Salesforce which will help you manage contacts and set up personalized email campaigns to nurture contacts and leads to conversion.

❯ SEM platforms like Google Ads that will enable your brand to show up in searches and rank high enough to get clicked on.

❯ Digital ads on social media sites like Facebook, Instagram, LinkedIn, TikTok, and media outlets covering your industry.

❯ Retargeting ad campaigns either using systems within the above platforms or an independent provider like AdRoll.

❯ Digital assets for building content to push out via the advertising channels you select. Your ads need to be linked to something meaningful to get engagement and if you can't write and produce content yourself, you'll need to invest in a content developer.

❯ Website builder and hosting services for your brand page. Your costs will be determined by the programs and functions you select, such as e-commerce features, payment processing, email addresses, and more. Many platforms such as GoDaddy, Squarespace, Wix, and more provide various options and customer service levels so you can purchase what you need and avoid features you don't.

❯ Design tools or freelance graphic designers are essential to your startup. You can use a low-cost service like Canva and build your own logo and brand iconology, or you can hire a professional to come up with something really unique.

〉 Another consideration as you get started is a publicity or a public relations professional. You need to be an authority in your space to get interviews, feature articles, speaking invitations for conferences, all of which are critical to get earned media mentions, the most credible and valuable type for establishing a new brand. If you have connections with media and conference planners, work your network. If you don't, it pays to hire someone who can work their network and is proven to get clients mentioned or featured in industry or general consumer media, on influencers' social pages, or speaking gigs at events.

〉 Miscellaneous needs: There are many tools to help you create, produce, and publish content such as stock image sites like Adobe Stock Images, Getty Images, and such to help you find compelling images for your digital assets; AI tools to help you write copy and produce videos, video editing platforms like VidYard, and so on. You will need to build a YouTube channel at some time which will require monthly subscriptions to manage and promote. You need content across platforms to engage with consumers how they want to be engaged with (e.g., white papers or video), so while you may not be able to afford everything at once, you need to keep these elements in mind as you plan ahead.

The key to budgeting is to set a budget you can grow with, set it up in a dynamic budget platform which automates calculations, set triggers to alert you about your actual spend vs. budget, and keep you focused on what you're spending. It's really easy to spend a little here and a little there, but that usually adds up to a lot somewhere you didn't plan to go.

Setting and Monitoring Metrics

A personal mantra of mine that has never let me down is: *If you can't measure it, you don't do it.* With all the instant access to digital dashboards that show the impact of our marketing efforts across all digital and social platforms, we can measure the impact of just about anything in real time. We can glimpse KPIs (Key Performance Metrics) that show which ads drive the most web traffic, the most clicks, generated the longest session durations, and lowest bounce rates. We can test different headlines on the same ad with A/B testing technology and see in real time which engaged targets best and which lead to the fastest path to conversion.

It's amazing what we can do with marketing technology today. And because of what we can do, there is no out for not measuring your results. If you don't, you will likely waste a lot of money and that is not a winning proposition for startups competing with established brands. Google Analytics will tell you in real time and over any time period you choose to review the number of users, new vs. old, where your audience or users are coming from, age and gender, what pages they landed on (you can set up different landing pages for your projects so you can monitor which drive the most traffic), and which pages users exited on. These are important metrics. These metrics will tell you which messages, blogs, videos, news articles, and other content on your website best engage and convert to Contact Us form completions or sales, two of your top metrics for website success.

Your CRM platform—HubSpot, Salesforce, and so on—will capture those Contact Us forms so you can monitor which activities and content tend to generate the most inquiries. These forms will also tell you about the source from which a given lead came. Google Analytics does a good job of this too, helping you see in real time which social ad platforms and the like drive the most website traffic and inquiries.

Your email service provider will also generate key metrics and KPIs for you. You get reports on open rates, click-through rates, bounces (so you can measure the quality of your database), and unsubscribes. Most platforms like MailChimp, Constant Contact, HubSpot, and others will let you conduct A/B tests so you can constantly measure what works and what does not.

You need to measure engagement and you need to measure your return on marketing investment, your ROMI. The first step is to know what to measure—what is meaningful and what is not. Impressions might be impressive, but unless they are among a very focused audience with a known propensity to purchase, you may be paying for a lot of non-qualified prospects to see your ad. If you are selling prom dresses, you don't want to waste your budget getting impressions among audiences that are not associated with purchasing prom dresses.

Finally, you need to stay on top of measuring your sales source, not just your lead source. Which distributors, salespeople, e-commerce sites are sending you the most revenue? Which channel generates the most leads that convert to customers? Are you getting enough from reseller partnerships, customer referrals? Is your in-house sales team meeting industry averages for quotas and closures? These are all elements you need to monitor closely to ensure the best use of your resources and funds.

GO TIME

Map out your marketing strategy so you can flesh out your thoughts on positioning, pricing, promotion, distribution, and what kind of research you need to stay on top of markets and consumers attitudes and needs for your category.

Keep this file open on your computer so you can refer to it and add to it constantly. Marketing is dynamic and new ideas will come to you constantly as you read more research, see more campaigns from others in your category or otherwise, and just learn more about your customers and what they expect.

Decide on a spreadsheet format for managing and monitoring your budget. Search online and see what you can find for free, and read reviews for ease of use, customer service, and functionality.

You don't need to manually document all the data from your marketing campaigns per the KPIs mentioned above, as you can find data by the date and source and other inputs instantly via your online systems. However, it makes sense to create a spreadsheet to record every ad, promotion, and event you do and document the returns like number of leads generated, inquiries from those leads, demos scheduled, proposals requested, sales conversions, and revenue generated. This will help you easily discover which messages, offers and channels work best and identify champions to repeat and refine.

CHAPTER 6

Building Your Brand with Content Marketing

Ads often fail to motivate behavior, especially in a market where many consumers do not trust advertisers. However, meaningful content designed to inform and involve consumers by sharing objective and useful information often does motivate consumers to engage with a brand. This is why content marketing is an important element of any successful marketing plan. You need to build marketing content that sets you apart from others in your space and positions you as the authority to follow and potentially do business with. This section will cover:

> Best types and formats for marketing content and how to most efficiently create it

> How to use content for high response marketing campaigns

> Ideas for spreading your content across different channels to spark meaningful conversations and SEO

> Tips for turning your website into a clearinghouse for actionable, information that builds trust and partnership value

> Content strategies and tactics for keeping your website fresh and inspiring visitors to linger longer

The best way to start this chapter is with a reality check. A fairly big one. As of this writing, those sponsored listings you keep seeing on Google search results pages have an average click-through rate of 0.46 percent for the advertisers paying thousands of dollars to be on the top of the rankings. While Facebook's click-through rate (CTR) is twice Google's, it still hovers below 1 percent. So when marketers see a 1 percent response, they get excited.

With brands projected to spend roughly $526 billion on digital marketing by year end 2024, mostly on Google and Facebook, according to a report released by WordStream in March 2024, it's hard for any entrepreneur to afford to jump into the game. And it really is just that. A game. If you want your ads to show up to the right people, you have to outbid others trying to reach the same audiences on the same channel. It takes constant monitoring of your keywords, adjusting your bids on keywords that align with your categories' top search queries, and then spending more than the other brand to get noticed in hopes that of all the thousands of impressions you create with your digital ads that the 0.4–0.9 percent of consumers that click on your ads will actually be qualified leads. And that those qualified leads will actually engage with your brand on your website so you can have a 10 percent chance to convert them. Whew. That's exhausting to think about, let alone write about. Oh, note to those of you in e-commerce, that sales conversion rate of 10 percent goes down to about 2–4 percent.

Engaging Customers Across Formats with Meaningful Content

The good news here is that you can up the odds if you develop better content than what is in a typical sponsored search listing, or Facebook display ad for your industry. If you make the time to understand the decision triggers and influencers of your customers, and the imminent challenges they face and solutions they seek, you can stand out and get a higher return on your ad efforts and spend.

The first step to developing good content is to understand what content is. Content refers to the elements you create to communicate your brand's positions, values, ESPs, about your products and promotions, and engage your customers and prospects with meaningful information that will help them achieve their goals. Content can be created in many formats and pushed out across many channels. Let's start with formats.

Formats driving engagement include:

Blogs	eBooks	Decision guides
Social media posts	Infographics	Social media ads
User generated content	Podcasts	Display ads
Customer stories	Presentations	Media pitches
Case studies	GIFs and memes	Press releases
White papers	Videos	

No, you don't need to create original content in each of the above formats. You do need to identify those most used by your targets and build compelling content accordingly. The key is to build content in the right formats around the right themes that will resonate quickly with your targets. Once you have a base piece, its fairly simple to create appropriate renditions for various formats like videos, e-books, display, and social that you can push out across the channels your targets use most.

Content themes that achieve the most engagement are those that provide educational information, not promotional appeals. Think about your own engagement patterns. When you see ads that shout, "Buy Now," without a good reason to do so you might just move on. In fact, many studies claim more than 50 percent of online display ads are ignored by consumers. On top of that big number, a Wordstream blog claims 94% percent of online searchers completely ignore the top lists on their Search Engine Results Pages (SERPs) that have the label "Sponsored" and instead click on the organic listings, non-sponsored ones, that get high rankings due to high levels of consumer engagement identified by search algorithms.

More and more, as evidenced by engagement rates and click-through rates and conversions, consumers refuse to be sold. They want to be informed, involved, and guided to wise choices that benefit them as much as their business benefits you. When it comes to budgeting your time for marketing, crafting relevant content should be among your top priorities. Without it, you're not going to get much in return for your marketing dollars. Developing a content marketing strategy is an investment in your brand with a high potential to pay off.

Crafting Relevant Content

When it comes to creating content, the format you use is secondary to the messaging, emotional appeal and personal value you present in each piece you produce. Marketing content needs to be viewed like a good novel. You need to emotionally connect your reader to your story in order to keep their attention and inspire them to continue to the end, or in business, get to the finish line. You just have a much shorter format to get to that point. Step one is to identify the topics that tap into the emotional triggers of choice among your customers. Examples of B2B and B2C marketing content follow.

B2B Content

If your customer is a purchaser of business systems, what emotions are associated with their decision process? Fear of hiring a vendor that does not deliver on promises which could set them up to miss executive and shareholder goals? This in turn could lead to fears about job security, maintaining the life they have, providing for families. It's a hot mess.

If the above applies, your content then will be most engaging if you build content that helps targets make good choices and takes the fear out of the decision process. Decision guides that provide actionable advice are most likely to get noticed. Some possible themes for a software or technology provider include:

> ❯ 5 Things to Look for in Technology Partners That Work for You

> ❯ Questions to Ask Before Choosing an ERP System

> ❯ Choosing the Right ERP System for Your Business: 7 Steps You Don't Want to Miss.

> ❯ 3 Mistakes to Avoid When Choosing a Technology Partner

If you produce content around helpful themes, you need to write objectively. You cannot create "educational" content that only educates readers about why they should buy from you. You need to guide people toward making good choices in your business category and write in a way that positions you as the authority, and thus the best choice for them.

B2C Content

Engaging consumers in a story that reflects what you can do for them can take on many different approaches. If you are in the fashion industry, you can create a Look Book to post on Instagram and other websites with new fashion trends, bridal looks, holiday styles to help you stand out, and more. You can create tips for helping your targets do what they already do well even better. Perhaps guides on how busy women can simplify their lives so they can be mom, wife, diva, girl boss, PTA president, neighborhood party planner, all at once (just kidding about this reality)! Examples of content that tend to get a lot of attention in the online world today include:

》 Tips for the Best Halloween Party in the Neighborhood

》 Turning Your Photo Hobby into a Profitable Business

》 3 Things Every Parent Should Know about Their Daycare Provider

Whatever themes you choose to develop, keep in mind the goal: instead of telling targets about your product and brand promises to start a relationship, tell them what they need to know to make wise choices, improve their lives, and what you can do for them. What you can do for them might be to elevate their sense of social status, self-worth, ability to self-actualize, all goals we humans are wired to achieve at some point in our lives, if not all the time. It might be helping them feel secure, tapping into their survival DNA socially, financially, or professionally. It might be about simplifying their lives with products or services that save time, reduce stress, or enhance well-being. Go back to your worksheets and find the ESPs you identified. Building content around your ESPs will help you rise above the average click-through and engagement rates no matter the industry in which you operate.

Using AI and Other Technology to Produce Content

After identifying themes, it's time to produce. This used to be the tricky part, but with the advent of AI and ChatGPT, this critical step is much easier. You don't have to be a prolific writer anymore. You just need to identify the key messages you want to convey with your theme, action items for readers to take to reach their goals, and then see what AI can come up with. Computers, at least in my opinion, are not smarter than humans despite some scientists stating otherwise. You will need to edit the copy to add some compelling messages about your brand's distinct values and outcomes, include some of your unique brand characteristics that ChatGPT won't include, and some tips that maybe the rest of the universe has not discovered yet which means ChatGPT can't spit it back in your content.

The challenge to keep in mind when using ChatGPT as your writing partner is that your copy will sound like everyone else's. It may be well written, it may flow logically and follow grammar rules, but it's not a unique voice to you. Use AI as a guide, not a final draft. You can add your voice and distinct brand messages, and imagery to an AI draft.

Of course other options are to hire a professional writer, or write content yourself. Just keep in mind, it needs to be written with an engaging, objective voice, and it needs to be persuasive. If this kind of writing is not in your wheelhouse, outsource your writing needs to someone who has a proven track record for content that captures attention and generates requests for information or sales conversations. There are numerous sites that can help match you with vetted content writers regardless of your industry. As of this writing, one of the leading sources is Contently which is used by many large Fortune 500 brands. Others include Upwork, Fiverr, and Composely. When hiring writers, take the time to read their samples so you can more efficiently find one that reflects the persona, style, and voice you want for your brand.

You can also download free "how-to" writing guides and templates for blogs, eBooks, press releases, brochures, case studies, and more from HubSpot, Microsoft, and others. Look to see what writing tools and templates your CRM system offers before investing time or money on other options.

After writing your content, you need to add design elements. You can't just publish a Word document and call it good. You need to add appeal through visuals that help tell your story. Again, you don't need to be a designer, and you don't even need to hire one. There are many sources for free and low-cost marketing templates you can customize for your content. Companies providing design templates for various content needs include Canva, Monday, Microsoft, and Adobe. However, one of the best and fastest ways to create content across reports, presentations, slide decks, and more is Beautiful.ai. It's just that. You put notes on a slide and the AI creates graphics and visuals to tell your story in a simple yet beautiful way. As an entrepreneur, this tool or another like it, can save you a lot of time and money, which is key for any startup.

Once you develop a theme, you need to produce it across various formats such as those listed earlier in this chapter. For example, if you produce content on creative children's party ideas and you sell "parties in a box" for busy parents, you may want to write up a party planning guide that can be downloaded on your website and produce a video on the same theme. If you, the entrepreneur, are the mind behind the ideas for the perfect party that comes in the mail, produce a video of you showing how easy it is to throw the perfect party with the right products. Include happy children in your video experiencing the kind of party only you can deliver. If you sell software to businesses, do a demo video with captures of your software in action, highlighting in real time how fast it is to accomplish routines tasks with your system.

Video is one of the most effective communications tools. Several studies show that the click-through rates on video ads are substantially higher than display ads. For video ads in mobile apps, a study by ad platform Smaato and app marketing firm Liftoff showed theclick-through rate was 7.5 times higher. Videos that explain what a product or service does and how it benefits customers have even more impressive stats. Research from Yans and Wyzowl in 2023 shows that landing pages for explainer videos convert 86 percent better, and 85 percent of those watching the video are more likely to buy a product. Another key statistic is that 68 percent of users prefer to watch an explainer video rather than talk to a brand representative who has been trained to sell them something before they get off the phone.

Video content does not have to be expensively produced. In fact, videos that are raw, feature real people, and have casual conversations with the viewers tend to engage better, project more authenticity, and better engage viewers for longer. The key is to keep them relevant and short. In fact, Idomoo, a personalized video production platform reported that the ideal length is 15–30 seconds. If you personalize a video, you can keep attention much longer. General and personalized videos are not expensive to produce anymore given what you can do with a smart phone and a free or low-cost video editor. Just search "Personalized Video Production Platforms" and compare vendors that catch your attention.

Just like for writing and design, there are AI video generator platforms as well. You just need to upload your script, or a pre-written blog, and the AI tools will create a video with footage, music, and text. In just seconds. Some of the leading platforms for AI video creation, per a Hubspot report include: Pictory, Synthesia, HeyGen, Deepbrain AI, and Synthesys. These are relatively inexpensive tools that will help you better engage your target audiences (again, video has one of the highest engagement rates), and boost your SEO as algorithms find video content as well as written content. For example, 2023 pricing for Pictory started at $19 a month for 30 videos, 2 million video snips to choose from, 5,000 music tracks, and a lot more. Maybe not the time right time now to expect to make a lot of money as a video producer, or even designer, for marketing content given the simplicity and low price for DIY technology.

User-Generated Content

One of the most powerful ways to tell your story is to let your customers tell it for you, from their unique experiences and lens. User-generated content (UGC) however, is not a new word for testimonials. It is just what it says—content your users create and post on social pages, yours and/ or theirs', showing them using your product. A LinkedIn article shared research showing that UGC is expected to grow more than 29 percent from 2023 to 2030. I'd plan on it growing even more as UGC is built upon authenticity which is something consumers increasingly demand and respond to much more than blatant advertising.

So, how do you get users to create content about their love for and experiences with your product and post it across social channels?

First, make a product worth talking about. Second, give them a reason. Starbucks' UGC campaign around their white cup was hugely successful and provides an example of a campaign that is affordable and easy to execute. They encouraged customers to buy a white Starbucks cup, draw all over it and submit their design to their White Cup Contest by posting it on their social media pages with the #WhiteCupContest hashtag. The winning design would become a new Starbucks cup available in stores. This campaign had more than 4,000 submissions from budding coffee cup artists, new revenue from sales from those who bought a cup to design, and quite a few impressions for the brand across multiple social channels.

Successful UGC campaigns do not need to include a contest, although contests do have a strong pull. Simply recognizing people for the life they live is a strong pull as well. People like to show off their style, their personalities, and like to be recognized for new ideas or achieving new feats. REI played on this with its REI challenges campaign which involved posting frequent challenges on its social pages to encourage followers to engage in more physical activities and outdoor adventures. For example, a challenge might be to record 250 minutes of activity in a given month. Each challenge is connected to the outdoor, adventurous lifestyle its products support. REI highlighted followers' entries and posts on Instagram and published leader boards, letting customers shine for living the life they love. Fun idea for building authentic stories around your business offerings, and creating loyalty among the customers you recognize.

UGC is a great way to get your social pages followed and build a community around your brand. Just make your asks of customers meaningful to them, not just you, and recognize them for posting stories about you.

Regardless of the format you use for your content—digital reports, slide decks, videos, blogs, etc.—your messaging needs to be spot on, your call to action easily actionable, and the content relevant for the channel. For example, if you push your content out across Facebook and Instagram, keep in mind your audiences are different, and so you may need to adapt it to be what each audience expects on each channel you use. TikTok a good channel for your audiences? Use a video generator to produce reels, and keep the content in line with the persona of TikTok viewers, which will be different than most Facebook users, and maybe even Instagram users.

Content Marketing Distribution Channels

Producing content and sending it out via your website and digital channels is not just a great way to position yourself as an authority in your space and a helpful partner to your customers, it is also a great way to boost your SEO rankings organically. The more content you have on your website with the keywords your customers use for search queries, the more chances you have of your website listing showing up on SERPs when you need it to.

The following are some ways you can get your content out to customers and the algorithms ruling the cyber universe.

Social Media

Posting content on social media channels and linking that content back to your website will help you get noticed for your expertise while introducing target customers to your brand. The process is similar across platforms. When posting on LinkedIn, your posts will do better when you include a visual or a video, and make your post about something valuable to the viewer. Your copy should be a short introduction to the value of the content followed by relevant hashtags. Here's an example of what you might post and tag on LinkedIn if you are posting a white paper to help product engineers choose robotic manufacturing partners.

Sample teaser copy to article on your website:

Do You Know the Top 3 Steps to Finding the Right Automation Partner for Your New Project? Here's a short checklist to help you get started.

Hashtags that may help your post show up in more LinkedIn users' feeds include: #automation, #robotics #manufacturing, #manufacturingintelligence, #manufacturingautomation, and so on. When you start tagging, LinkedIn and other platforms often auto finish the hashtag and shows you how many searches are currently associated with that hashtag. When you see search terms with no numbers by it, you are not likely to increase your reach with those words.

If you're selling B2C products, like organic skin care for acne treatment, you'd do well to post a teaser on your Facebook page showing before and after results for users, and linking it directly to your website with keywords like #acnetreatment, #organicskincare #affordableskincareprod-ucts, and so on. It's important for your content to contain the keywords that show up with the most searches for the channels you use. Per the B2B example above, if you find that #manufacturingautomation has a lot of queries on LinkedIn, and on Google or Bing searches, make sure that term shows up a few times in your copy and use it in your headline. When you post content on your website, tag the backend of your page, meta and title tag forms accordingly.

Email Campaigns

Whether you are using Constant Contact, Mailchimp, HubSpot, or Salesforce, the quality of your email content is one of the biggest contrib-utors to your success.

The key to successful email campaigns is to send out content that is highly relevant to your recipients, objective, and actionable. Your content marketing emails should be educational in tone and offer free reports, checklists, how-to videos, and the like. Content should be inserted as a link to the page on your website where it lives, not as an attachment. Email with attachments will often end up in spam, and many firewalls won't let mass emails with attachments go through. By linking content in your email to your website, you are also driving traffic to your site where visitors can see more information about what you can do for them, leading to inquiries or sales transactions.

There are many email marketing service providers that offer similar tools, but at very different price points. It pays to review your options and find one you can afford now that will allow you to upgrade your account as you grow. As of this writing, Mailchimp is one of the highest rated options for personalized email campaigns for small businesses and is priced exponentially lower than the category leaders HubSpot and Salesforce. Something to keep in mind is the level of support you will have access to for the price you pay. HubSpot is expensive, but the instant access to support to help you troubleshoot and set up campaigns, contact lists, and more can be worth the price for some.

Third-Party Websites

Getting your content posted on other's websites is huge for getting noticed and building credibility. Among the most influential third-party sites are media sites. Industry media organizations are often short staffed and looking for objective content they can post to keep readers coming back. Sending content about your business developments, product releases, leadership team, and actionable content such as checklists and how-to tips can often get you mentioned on sites that have thousands of visitors a month. If you embed a link to your website in your content, you create a backlink which makes your site show up higher in SEO organically. Additionally, your brand's presence on a media site adds credibility for your market position and thought leadership. Mentions and links on influencers' websites and social pages will have the same type of impact, so browse the web for people posting about your space on channels such as YouTube, X, Instagram, and more, and send them your content to use.

YouTube is another third-party website you need to work into your content marketing plan. Creating a YouTube channel for your brand costs nothing and can deliver a lot of SEO results and exposure to new consumers. YouTube gets a lot of visitors for various reasons, one of which is because it is owned by Google, which means it has a lot of algorithm activity. You can also use YouTube for affordable retargeting, a tactic discussed later on in this book.

Using Content-Based Campaigns to Build Your Customer Database

Your content marketing is only as successful as your ability to deliver your content to key targets. Beyond reaching target audiences through social media, you need to build a database of qualified prospects and customers to which you can email your content with the ultimate goal of building connections and conversations.

Creating meaningful content is not just for engaging consumers with your brand, it is also largely for building your database and powerful network. Your content should be viewed as a powerful tool for attracting prospects to your brand and securing permission to market to them which helps you build an email list of qualified leads. There are a few paths to use content to build your email database.

Spark Email Conversations

For one, list an email address in all pieces you produce and on all channels you use for content distribution so that interested prospects can reach out to you via email directly. Doing so gives you an opportunity to start a conversation directly and gives you their email address so you can reach out to get permission to send them future emails or invite them to sign up for updates or newsletters.

Set Up Subscriptions for Your Content

Newsletters are still a good format to use for your content as they require people to subscribe to receive them monthly or however often you send them out. And subscriptions require email addresses for delivery, giving you more to add to your permissioned database. The key to newsletters is to keep them short and actionable, not promotional, and to incentivize subscribers to share with others who may benefit from subscribing. There are numerous templates available, for free, to help you create a digital newsletter that aligns with how people read today.

Require Registration

Create a resource page on your website to house your white papers, decision guides, industry briefs, and such, and consider asking people to register on your website to download your content. This can be a turn off to some, but if your content is worthwhile, research shows more people will give you their email address and contact information in order to access it. If you keep it objective, educational, informative, and how-to in nature, your chances for qualified registrants will go up. If you do this, set your content up so that a compelling summary is readable before requiring registration for those who want to read further. Once someone has given you their email address, it goes into your Contacts folder on your CRM and from there can be added to a database for future permissioned communications. Building your email lists from people that have shown interest in your brand and what you have to say is far more successful and profitable than purchasing lists of customers that you end up spamming if they have not given you permission to market to them. Keep content like news features, press releases, archived newsletters and articles, and business updates available without registration. Content people will most likely register for include how-to guides, proprietary research, industry analytics and projections, and other material that is timely and actionable,

Getting prospects into your CRM system and database paves the way for future personalized communications, which will be far more effective than your generic marketing programs. Most CRM systems will alert you when someone in your contacts database visits your website and engages with your content, giving you an opportunity to reach out and spark individual conversations, which ultimately is the goal of all content marketing. And all marketing for that matter.

As you build your database of consumers for your email marketing, ask for permission to text them about special promotions, order status, and to communicate with them via text marketing, which is another successful form of communication. You can give them the option of opting in for future communications, or you can automatically enroll them and give them the option of opting out. Either way, to adhere to industry standards for privacy and anti-spamming, you need to provide options for no longer receiving emails from your brand.

GO TIME

Browse websites for media and influencers in your industry to identify topics that have the most engagement. Look for likes, shares, impressions, and any other metric you can access. Document these topics in your Marketing Plan grid as hot topics that capture the attention (at least for the moment) of the groups and individuals you need to target.

Highlight topics in which you or a member of your team are a SME. Outline discussion points you can add to the existing narrative on the web. Can you add user stories, case studies, tips for saving money or accelerating performance, productivity, or industry insights?

Set up a process for creating content. Are you going to use AI via a platform like Canva to help you write, design, and distribute reports, how-to guides, checklists, and both digital and video versions of the topics you choose to build out?

Build a list of media representatives and industry influencers to whom you can send your educational content pieces. Ask them to include your material on their sites and offer interviews with your SMEs for further story angles. You will use this same list for establishing your thought leadership presence, making it pay off even more.

Post your content on your social media pages. For example, post technical tips for B2B audiences on LinkedIn, entertaining reels on TikTok, bold posts about your brand on Facebook and Instagram. Link to the landing page on your website so that readers can find it immediately (they'll likely bounce otherwise), and monitor the time on your landing pages for each piece of content, the exit pages for those entering your content pages, and inquiries generated to help you identify future topics likely to pay off better than others. Join groups on each of your platforms and post your content on group pages, not just your own, to expand your reach.

Decide how you will send your content to prospects to expand your reach beyond the customers you already have in your email database. Will you ask for registration to add email addresses to your database? Can you ask partners to send your content to their email lists which enables you to add email addresses of anyone responding to your content from those lists to your own list?

Look for new avenues and networks to get your content as far and deep in the circles you serve as possible.

CHAPTER 7

Building Leads with Social Media and Digital Marketing

Social media can be and often is the never-ending dark hole of wasted time. Yet it is a critical channel for building brands, customer databases, and sales leads. With many channels offering sales functions for brands, not just entertaining or promotional posts, it's more and more important to understand how your customer base uses these platforms and how you can capture attention and sales accordingly.

This chapter will cover tips for turning social media posts into web traffic and sales across various channels including:

- Facebook
- LinkedIn
- Instagram
- TikTok
- Google Profile

You will also learn about purchasing and producing digital ads, including how to optimize your budget for purchasing ads or mentions on websites that attract your customer base. You'll learn about:

- Identifying the best websites, newsletters, trade magazines, and other channels for your digital advertising
- Creating ads that get noticed and clicked on
- Getting ROI for ads and sponsored content on social platforms like Facebook, LinkedIn, and media sites

The reason this book and so many other business books in the present, the recent past, and in the future will focus on "marketing" not "advertising" is because advertising alone no longer works. It did in the days of Lester Wunderman and other pioneers of the trade, and before ads permeated every aspect and event of our lives. The lack of recall and response for most "advertising" today compared to the "old days" has helped marketing evolve as a strategic relationship function focused on long-term customer value over a sales strategy to spark immediate sales. The key to building relationships that lead to long-term customer value is not more ads promising *Buy One Get One 50% Off, Limited Time Only* offers, it's about providing meaningful content that simplifies or enhances the lives of your customers—just like we discussed in Chapter 6.

Assuming you have read Chapter 6 on content marketing, this chapter expands on methods and processes to distribute your content across various social media channels, and how to set up efficient paid and unpaid media programs programs on these channels as well, including Facebook, LinkedIn, Instagram, TikTok, Google Ads, and more. The best channels for you to use depends on the kind of business you operate, and where your target customers hang digitally to get connected, informed, or entertained. Because so many of our human connections, personal and professional, are online connections only, and our real worlds and online worlds don't often collide, building a plan for expanding your online social circles and engaging your connections in meaningful ways is critical to your business success. Your plan needs to identify themes that will most resonate with your targets, how frequently you will post what you can afford to pay for content exposure, and how you will respond to people commenting and sharing your posts.

Social Media Strategies for Top Channels

Marketing on social media channels is all about content that captures attention quickly, engages the conscious and unconscious mind in a relevant story, and inspires viewers to learn more about the post. Each time you post on your social media pages, your goal should be to spark interest in your topic, your expertise, and your brand, and inspire viewers to engage by liking, commenting, and best of all, clicking on the hotlink that takes them to your website or e-commerce store. The challenge is that one post does not fit all channels. The content you post must align with the persona of the channels and the persona of the users of each channel.

Back to the nutrition bar example, if your business is making and selling organic nutrition bars, you may have two stories to post about. The first story could detail how your bars help pump up a run, hike, bike ride, or other sports events; and the second could describe how your bars are good for snacking and more nutritious than a candy bar for your hangry moments. For both of these stories, you could include much of the same information about your ingredients and the mental and physical boost they provide. However, when it comes to posting on different social channels, you will likely gain more engagement if you adapt the tone and format of each story to fit the persona of each channel and its subsequent users. For TikTok, you may have a 15-second reel showing a runner accelerating while eating your protein bar; another with young adults snacking while watching TV. For Facebook, you could show images of business executives snacking at their desk, or post a link to a quiz designed to help young parents choose the right bar for their kids' daily activities. And, on LinkedIn, you would change the story altogether and post links to reports on your website about your growing business, investment opportunities, and the role you play in the growing nutrition industry.

With millions of users engaging with posts, ads, and reels across the primary social channels, there are infinite opportunities to use social media for building brand awareness and online networks of potential customers and influencers. The key is to keep your content about the user more than about your products so that viewers will want to follow your pages to learn more valuable insights on ways to reach their own goals or improve their lives. The ultimate goal of social media marketing is to get viewers to follow your posts back to your website where they embark on a journey with your brand from introduction to trial to loyal customer.

While there are many formats you can use for your social posts, there are primarily two methods for marketing: organic and paid. The most used channels for social media today, Facebook, Instagram, LinkedIn, and such, offer opportunities to grow networks through both organic and paid programs.

Organic Social Media

Organic social media activities refer to the content you create and post on your pages without paying for greater distribution than what results from those following your pages and those that come via the hashtags and keywords you use. To expand your reach organically, you need to use a lot of keywords, hashtags, and post content frequently. A good approach is to post short but compelling teasers to the blogs, articles, videos, and more on your website, increasing traffic and setting yourself up to capture emails and thus permission for further engagement via marketing channels.

The following are some examples of organic social media for B2C and B2B brands.

Facebook

Although grocery stores are a pretty stable staple, they still engage in social media to build networks within their communities and customer loyalty. Here's a fun example of how a grocery chain engages its consumer communities with Facebook. King Soopers is a large grocery chain serving communities in the Rocky Mountain Region. Their Facebook page has more than 120,000 followers who can see posts about recipe ideas, food prep tips, lunch box ideas, charcuterie suggestions, how to use Halloween candy leftovers, and other content you would expect from a food store. Their content is posted in various forms, static posts, content with photos, videos and reels. However, King Soopers does not stop with the expected content about food items, coupons, special deals for special occasions, and such. They engage customers, pretty much all food eaters, with heartwarming content that helps them feel good about the brand. A post which quickly became one of my favorite business posts was one posted November 17, 2023 that showed what happened when 30 strangers were invited to bring a favorite dish and share dinner with each other. It shows the power of food for connecting people, the joy of companionship, the bonding of strangers who would otherwise not likely notice each other much, and of course the power of heartwarming posts on social media.

As an entrepreneur, consider how you can bring people together around your product to build connections, share stories, share usage ideas for your product pre and post launch, and just feel good about the world for a day or two. It does not cost much to host a small event, record it on your smartphone, and then post snippets about your event and the resulting outcomes. A post about people enjoying life around your product is likely to get more people wanting to be part of your brand circles. Start imagining people coming together over your products and your promises, and then find a way to make some of what you visualize happen.

HubSpot's Facebook page does a really good job of engaging its 1.2 million plus followers. They post reels, videos, and static content that all get a decent amount of likes, shares, and comments. Some of their posts are entertaining, others are case studies that show the impact of their software on nurturing and converting leads, and others are just meant to engage, like a post that simply asked, "How many tabs do you have open right now?" A question and quirk to which many can relate.

Salesforce posts frequently on Facebook to let its nearly one million followers know about new features, products, case studies, and events. Its content is frequent, recent and fresh, and gets strong engagement for most of its posts, well into the tens of thousands for some. All posts link back to a page on Salesforce's main website that builds on the story, which is key to building relationships and capturing emails and potential sales via social media.

Ogilvy, one of the world's largest and most renowned ad agencies, has more than 500,000 followers on Facebook, and around two million connections on LinkedIn. Ogilvy's team mostly posts its ads, case studies, and employee and business news. They mix their posts up with some great quotes from their founder, David Ogilvy, one of my favorites of which is "You aren't advertising to a standing army. You are advertising to a moving parade." Take that one to heart.

Success on Facebook for both B2C and B2B brands is dependent on posting engaging content that is meaningful to your followers, staying present on your page to respond to posts and participate in conversations, and directing viewers of your posts to your website where they can get more information and hopefully complete a Contact Us form which gives you a path to a personal conversation.

LinkedIn

Although LinkedIn has seen an increase in personal posts in recent years, it's still the gold standard and leading platform for networking with business peers and target prospects. Most companies post business news, product updates, jobs, personnel news, and highlights from events they hosted or tradeshows they attended. LinkedIn was started as a networking platform where business executives can go to learn about new things and network with others for business relationships, job searches, and learning. With its 950 million members as of this writing, it's an important place for posting content about your brand and your expertise as a SME (subject matter expert) in your field. Content that shares how-to guidance, industry updates and breakthroughs, and new ideas will help you build a network and generate leads the fastest on LinkedIn. For example, checklists like "3 Steps to Choosing the Right CRM Partner" tend to get a lot of likes and clicks and shares, the metrics of success on LinkedIn, all of which will help your brand get noticed within your own network and those of others sharing your content.

As a member of LinkedIn, you can join LinkedIn groups which are pages set up to create dialogue among people in like industries or with similar business goals. Joining these groups immediately expands your network and reach. Posting objective and informative content on the pages of LinkedIn groups associated with your industry is a simple and effective way to get more exposure and ultimately followers for your own page. If you post promotional links on group pages, it will not only result in little to no interaction, it could result in your getting booted from a given group. As you establish expertise in your space, consider starting your own group which will position you as a SME to others on LinkedIn and likely connect you with people you would not be introduced to otherwise.

The key to succeeding on LinkedIn is to post content that educates others about your industry, how to make wise and informed decisions, and your business achievements that are relevant to your various audiences. This is a critical playing field for B2B companies who need to create a presence in their field, increase familiarity among partners, generate leads, and catch the attention of potential investors.

For LinkedIn, you will want to post both videos and static posts about your products, your brand, your personnel, and partnerships. Be personable and showcase who you are as an inventor, entrepreneur, and human with your posts and the content you develop about your category.

Even if you are a B2C brand, creating a business network is important, especially if you seek partners or investors at some point. A consumer retailer's LinkedIn page may have posts about business news, new products, organizations they support, and news that partners, investors, and fans alike will appreciate. Another reason to be on LinkedIn if you are not a B2B brand is the SEO you get from having a presence on a highly visited website, and your URL on a platform where others can like your posts and follow your links.

Instagram and TikTok

Both Instagram and TikTok cater to the younger generations of consumers who use these platforms mostly to be entertained, or to entertain others. And both deliver content that can be consumed quickly—in an instant—Instagram, or the tick of a second on a clock—TikTok. Short, really short videos are a common format used on both channels. Instagram also allows for images without a lot of text as is allowed on its sister platform, Facebook. On either channel, be prepared for lots of impromptu dancing and cute pet posts.

Especially if your business targets consumers over business purchasers, it is important not to ignore either of these channels as they have large followings, and large influence over those that use them. It's also important to post content that fits the persona of these channels frequently so that the algorithms can find you and show your reels or images to more followers more regularly. Spend some time on these channels to see what people are posting, what people are following, liking and sharing, and more. Then build out a content plan for getting noticed among the users you want to reach. The key is relevant content that fits the style of the posts most liked on each channel, and fits the personality and needs of the users from which you need to capture attention.

To use these platforms most effectively, post with relevancy and frequency. The more likes you get for your entertaining or intriguing content, the more algorithms find you and present you in search queries, and the more people you are likely to get to your website where you can better inform them and inspire conversations.

To optimize the return on posting content across these channels, and any social media channel for that matter, means generating high volumes of views, comments, shares, and likes. Your goal should not be to promote sales as much as to get people talking about the value, quality, innovations, or emotional fulfilment of your products and brand experience. However, like Facebook and LinkedIn, you can advertise on Instagram and TikTok to help boost your brand's visibility and more rapidly grow followers.

Paid Social Media

As a new business, it's hard to trigger the algorithms of any social media platform in your favor as a lot of those triggers are based on a prolonged history of advertising and posts with comments and shares. But trigger you must, as these channels engage billions of monthly active users (MAUs) and cannot be ignored by any business—small, large, startup, or established. Take a look at the numbers:

Monthly Active Users as of November 2023

- Facebook   3.03 billion
- YouTube   2.5 billion
- WhatsApp   2 billion
- Instagram   2 billion
- TikTok   1.5 billion
- LinkedIn   310 million

As a small business owner, you need to join the fray of advertisers trying to reach these MAUs with a collective $173 billion USD spend in social media advertising in 2022. This number is expected to rise to $270 billion for 2023 and $385 billion in USD in 2025, per Hootsuite, a social media management platform which provides users a dashboard for managing multiple programs simultaneously. Advertising on social media in addition to maintaining organic posts substantially helps launch a brand's presence and number of followers more quickly than relying on organic growth alone. According to data provided by Meta, parent company for Facebook, social media advertising works. Meta's data reports that for Instagram and Messenger alone, 69 percent of users say a social media ad sparked them to make a purchase, and 61 percent say a social media ad inspired them to try a new brand. These are not numbers to ignore.

Tips to Keep Advertising Affordable

Setting up advertising on social media channels is similar across all platforms. The main steps include:

> **Determining your goals:** Most platforms assist you in creating ads that align with specific goals such as awareness, form completion, event registration, website traffic, and so on. You choose and set your conversion metric in the platform as you set up your ads which makes it easy for you to monitor how much you pay for each conversion.

> **Setting a budget:** Once you choose your goal, you can input the amount you want to spend over a given period of time. For example, $100 a day over 5 days, two weeks, or more. Because you can increase, decrease, or turn off an ad campaign at any time, instantly, social media is a great testing ground to see which incentives, promotions, and messages drive the most engagement and goal achievement without spending a lot of money. Test results come back quickly and you can easily and instantly shift budgets to the campaigns that are performing and stop the ones that are not.

> **Creating ads:** With AI, creating ads on social platforms is faster and easier than before, and does not require skills in graphic design or even copywriting. You can create ads that deliver personalized communications or general messages for general audiences, and you can automate entire campaigns to keep your ads moving without a lot of effort or time on your part. As discussed throughout this book, your ads will only be as good as the emotional and functional relevance you include and the appeal of your incentives and promises.

❯ **Targeting your audience:** Social media platforms enable you to pay to reach just the audiences you need to reach, and avoid wasting money on those you don't, optimizing the potential return on your investment. These platforms allow you to create audiences in a variety of ways:

- A custom audience that could include people already following or interacting with your page, those having visited your website from your social media pages or mobile communications, and so on.

- Lookalike audiences are those that are built by the platform algorithms and consist of people with similar interests and demographics to those listed in your account profile. If you have conversion pixels set up in your social media accounts, you can create audiences similar to those that have engaged with your page or converted to whatever conversion metric you set up, e.g., schedule a call, complete a form, visit your website, and so on.

- Saved audiences are those that you save in your account so you can use them for future campaigns. Audiences you save should be those that have been identified to have the demographics, interests, and behaviors most likely to convert to being a customer.

❯ **Publishing:** Once you set up your campaign per the above elements, you are then ready to schedule your ads to be published across a given platform for the time period and budget you have established. It's important to review your dashboard frequently to monitor the return on your ads and identify champions vs. lack luster ads so you can learn what personas, appeals, offers, headlines, and themes are most likely to pay off the most over time.

❯ **Monitoring:** Frequently reviewing the information provided by your social media advertising dashboards is critical for optimizing your spend and for learning more about customer interests and behavior. As Meta gets the most ads across social media, here's what you can learn from your Meta dashboard:

- **Delivery:** This tells you if your ad campaign is active, pending, paused, or complete.
- **Bid strategy:** This is where you see how your bids for keywords are working, or not. You can set a cost cap for specific keywords, a bid cap for automated bidding by Meta, and set your targets for cost and ROAS—return on advertising spend. This column will tell you how well your strategies are working.
- **Budget:** Your budget is shown to you by amount spent per day during your set campaign, and over the lifetime of your campaigns.
- **Attribution:** This column shows the time period you selected for conversion, which is then the period during which conversions will be credited. For example, if you selected a 7-day click strategy, Meta will report conversions in that time period and will automatically show your ads to Meta platform users that have a history of converting in that same time period.
- **Results:** This will show you the desired outcomes you achieved during your campaign—clicks, responses, visits to website, etc.
- **Reach:** This is an important metric to monitor. Reach refers to the number of people in your account profile that saw your ad. This numbers accounts for one view per person reached and is not the same as impressions.
- **Impressions:** This is the metric for how many times your ad appeared on a screen and includes one person seeing that ad multiple times. Knowing how many of the right audience members you reached is more important than paying for a lot of impressions among people who are not fits for your product or brand. The number of impressions is far less important than the number of clicks you generate.
- **Cost per result:** Monitoring how much you paid for each click, web visit, or form completion is important for managing

your resources. If you are paying $100 per result, your revenue potential must be higher for you to drive a profit. You can search for benchmarks for costs per results, per action, and so on across industries to see what is standard for your industry.

- **Amount spent:** The last column helps you monitor a running total for what you are spending to achieve the data shown to you in the previous columns, and is important to monitor so you can best use the money you have to spend, and compare Meta channels to others like TikTok and LinkedIn.

Advertising on TikTok and LinkedIn follows a similar process. Set your goals, create an ad or ad campaign, go live, and monitor. You need to choose the social media platform best suited for your business and key targets, set up an account, and test ideas for ads, copy, incentives, offers, headlines, images, videos, and so on until you find those that perform the best. Modeling future ads against your champions will save you a lot of money and headaches as you grow.

Mass advertising, digital or print ads that reach large and varied audiences, create a lot of waste when they generate views among audiences that have no relevance for your products or brand. Again, this is why you should not measure impressions of your ads across channels as much as the engagement you receive. It does not matter if you, or an ad agency you hire, generate 1 million users a month if only 10 percent of those impressions are among people that actually have an interest in your product. When this happens, you have wasted 90 percent of what you spent on those impressions.

Getting Personal with SMS, MMS, and OTT Communications

In marketing there is no shortage of acronyms you need to understand, three of which are SMS, MMS, and OTT. The real simple explanation is that collectively they are all forms of Text Messaging and individually they differ as follows:

SMS—Short message service that is delivered in a text message to a device receiving cellular data, e.g., your cell phone.

MMS—Multi-Media Messaging which is a text-based message like SMS, but includes a file, like a link to a website page, an image, even an emoji.

OTT—Refers to Over the Top messaging and is messaging over a platform that requires an Internet connection, like WhatsApp,, Facebook Messenger, Google Business messaging, and the like.

The common ground is that all three of these options are a form of messaging which can be hyper-personalized, e.g., "Your flight is boarding," or "Items in your shopping cart have been reduced in price," and sent in mass. According to statistics shared on Twilio.com, a leading CPaaS (Communications Platform as a Service Provider) in 2023, the results of text messaging using these methodologies are pretty powerful:

〉 98 percent open rate

〉 90 percent are read within 3 minutes of being received

〉 45 percent response rate

While these are impressive, keep in perspective that more than 130 billion marketing text messages are sent and received via Twilio's platform annually. Beyond Twilio, many CRM platforms also offer text messaging so check your CRM to see if you have this feature before investing in another subscription with another company. Some of the CRMs with messaging options include brands you've likely heard of like MailChimp and HubSpot, but also others not as well known. According to Minterapp, an online service designed to help freelancers and small businesses manage projects and operations, some of the current CRMs with messaging services for small business include SalesMate, Bitrix24, AgileCRM, Freshworks. These lists will change frequently and so will their pricing so Google Small Business CRMs with Text Messaging to get the latest lists of leading platforms that include text messaging so you can compare the value of a CRM's tools vs. a pureplay CPaaS like Twilio.

Digital Marketing beyond Google

There is more to digital advertising than the ads put out on Google Ads and social media channels. There are many websites for organizations serving your brand's community and your industry at large that are worth spending your ad budget on. If you own a restaurant, a local floral or other type of retail shop, or a financial consulting, tax preparation firm, consider buying ads on local websites such as your chamber of commerce, community newspaper's digital page, even local school district's pages, and more. There are far more opportunities to reach local audiences that are inexpensive and enable you to reach precisely the audiences you are looking to serve.

If you are a B2B business serving a specific industry or niche, look up the trade media and associations that cover your world and browse options they have for advertising to the members they reach with their website and newsletters. on their website each month. These can include but are not limited to:

> ❭ Newsletters in which you can place banner ads or sponsored content such as editorials you write that are inserted much like articles written by staff editors. The visual difference between your ad and a staff article might just be the "sponsored" tag in small print. Sponsored content, or editorials you write yourself, can be quite effective as long as your article is written objectively and reads like news, not a promotion.

> ❭ Some trade media will even create a custom newsletter for your brand that features articles you write and submit to them, and send that newsletter to their database of superscribers/visitors to their own page.

> ❭ Banner ads on trade media sites are available in various sizes and for various locations. You will pay by the size and placement of your banner, e.g., large home page masthead, or a smaller sidebar on a secondary page. These typically do not get a lot of response; however, they can at least get your name out there and increase awareness so your ads in other places, for example your booths at tradeshows, and your SEO listings, reflect familiarity which as we discussed in earlier chapters is key to growing a brand.

⧽ Podcasts and webinars are another option trade media might offer brands in their space. You can pay to be interviewed on a podcast, featured as a SME (subject matter expert) on a webinar, or you can sponsor episodes for either format featuring authorities such as professors, researchers, and influencers in your field.

Advertising on trade media websites is not a low-cost endeavor in many cases, so spend time looking at media kits for all publishers in your space. Pay attention to monthly active users (MAUs, a term discussed earlier for social media channels), impressions, audience demographics, and average ROAS (return on advertising spend) and conversions for other advertisers. Going back to the value of customer surveys, it can help you use your budget wisely if you set up a one-question survey on your website or a social media page to ask what media outlets your customers browse, read, and follow the most. Knowing what they read and visit most often can help you get the most out of advertising vs. guessing which ones best reach your best targets.

GO TIME

Before you can set up successful digital, organic or paid social media campaigns, you need to craft messaging that shows how your brand really stands out according to the values and ESPs discussed earlier. Take the time to create your messaging strategy, which will inform much of your paid advertising choices moving forward.

Identify the keywords most related to your messaging, brand, category, and search queries by targeted audiences. Having a messaging strategy in place will enable you to more easily prioritize the keywords you need to bid on and use throughout your content, and identify advertising outlets that support your messaging.

Research the channels (e.g., Facebook, LinkedIn, TikTok) most used by your target audiences. Look for the most viewed and liked topics and formats to give you an idea of what will likely work best for your own posts.

Craft content according to the information you gather from above activities and set up a schedule in your Excel spread sheet marketing plan for getting that content out organically and via paid ads.

Map out your budget for advertising and allocate it across social media pages, Google Ads, local and trade website ads, and retargeting. Allocate your funds according to the channels where most of your customers spend most of their time. You can learn this through secondary research available about consumer use of social and trade media, and by asking customers when they spend their time online, how they heard about you, and which channels influence them the most.

CHAPTER 8

Creating Sticky Websites

It goes without saying that your website is your most valuable asset. It is the go-to tool for anyone wanting to learn about what you offer, how you compare to others, the values you stand for and live by, and what you can do for them. The presentation of your story on your website, the visuals and words you use, matters a lot if you want to keep people from bouncing in less than a second, or engaged enough to scroll past the first paragraph and keep going long enough and deep enough to want more information.

This chapter will share:

> Examples of websites that are crushing it for keeping people engaged and coming back

> Tips and ideas for building a sticky website that moves users from your landing page to asking for more information or a shopping cart transaction

> An overview of current website building tools to make it easier to do it yourself than you may think

> SEO tips for getting your website noticed in searches for your products and category

The point of social media, organic and paid digital marketing, and all marketing programs for that matter, is to drive people to your website where you can engage them in meaningful brand journeys from your landing page to a shopping cart or request for sales meeting. As so much of the decisions we make as consumers or B2B purchasers are influenced by websites we visit, building a site that is compelling and delivers a high quality, engaging and meaningful user experience is one of the most important things any entrepreneur can do. If your website does not engage visitors with the information they went there to find within 5 seconds, 61 percent will go to another site according to a Forbes report in 2023. This presents a brutal reality:

If your website lacks a clear user experience,
direct relevance to users, engaging copy and design,
and a simple navigation process, your marketing efforts are for not.

The good news is that with AI and other design technology, building engaging websites is not all that difficult, time consuming, or expensive. But selecting a website builder to help you create a web brand presence is not the first step in creating your brand's most visible and engaged asset. Building a solid strategy for your website presentation and user experience is. Your website strategy needs to be built around delivering a relevant, comprehensive, and simple user experience backed by strategic design and copy crafted to appeal to user personas, and lead visitors on pathway to the conversion you desire such as registering for an event, completing a sales demo request form, or asking for more information. Your website also needs to execute interactions that are worth coming back for.

Web Statistics You Can't Ignore

Here's some statistics to get you thinking as you start mapping out your plan for a successful website. You can view many of these statistics in the Forbes 2023 report on website viewing data found here https://www .forbes.com/advisor/business/software/website-statistics/.

> ❯ As of 2023, there were around 1.13 billion websites across the world wide web. If that is alarming, note that 82 percent of these were

inactive, which means you are operating in a universe of closer to 200,121,724 other sites. (Source: Sitefly).

❯ The average click-through rate on a landing page to the call to action, e.g., adding items to a shopping cart, scheduling a demo, or completing a Contact Us form is 4.23 percent (VYE agency). The better the copy, design, and relevance of your landing page, the better your chances are for increasing this statistic.

❯ Users form an opinion about a website in about 0.05 seconds, down from 3 seconds a few years ago. Your design and headline copy have a lot to do with that opinion so spend time getting these critical elements right (Google Search and SparkToro).

❯ 93 percent of all web traffic globally comes from Google Ads and search engine marketing, making this a necessary tool in all businesses' toolkits (SparkToro).

❯ 51.2 percent of web traffic globally comes from mobile devices (Statista).

❯ Conversion rates for e-commerce sites range between 1.81 percent to 3.71 percent (Geckoboard).

❯ On average, users that don't bounce quickly spend 5.59 seconds looking at a site's copy (CXK).

❯ 6.44 percent of seconds are spent on average looking at a site's navigation menu (CXL).

❯ 54 seconds is the average time spent on a website (Hubspot) which means you need to be quick to communicate what you deliver to users that matters to them and why you're better than alternative options.

❯ Videos on a website increase time spent by 88 percent. (Animato). According to Wistia, time spent on pages with videos soars to an average of 6 minutes, a huge bump from the 54 seconds reported above by HubSpot.

❯ Average bounce rate is 41–55 percent for websites across industries, meaning the engagement rate is between 45–59 percent (Search Engine Journal). Your target engagement rate should be 50 percent or higher.

❯ Perhaps one of the biggest statistics to keep in mind is this: 61 percent of users will go to another website in your category if they can't find what they are looking for in just 5 seconds (Forbes article on viewing statistics). Again, simple and quick access to the information about your products, locations, pricing and information frequently sought by website visitors is key to getting the most out of your website and converting visitors to qualified leads.

❯ Another statistic that should be a driving factor in your copy strategy is that 57 percent of time spent on a page is before the fold, or the need to scroll to see what's below the "fold," or the upper half of a landing page (Neilsen Norman Group study).

What these statistics tell us in short is simply:

❯ Your design matters. It needs to showcase your brand's innovation, alignment with current technology and market trends, and it needs to appeal to the persona of your target user. We do business with brands that reflect our values and desires just like we seek to associate with people that reflect who we are socially and intellectually.

❯ Your copy needs to immediately reference what visitors are looking to achieve by going to your website, and they need to be able to find the pages or resources they are looking for quickly. Actually, pretty much immediately.

❯ Copy blocks with lots of text are not going to make your page sticky, another term for websites that keep people on a site, and going deeper than the initial landing page. You need videos, informative content, interactive elements, and reasons to go deeper onto a page to add items to a shopping cart or register for a sales demo.

❯ Your most important messages, the content users seek, and the hooks to get them to stay longer and delve deeper need to be above the need to scroll, or what they can see on the top half of your page.

Engaging Visitors with Your Story

The strategy behind your site is not something you should put together hastily. To start, you need to move away from the oh-so-common mindset that a website is a digital brochure to promote your products, services, promises, customer satisfaction, and success stories. Instead, think of your website as a tool for sparking conversations and buildling relationships that are more valuable than just the desired transactions between two parties. Think of how you go about making big purchases in your own life, personal and professional. Most of us do not go to one website, instantly find a product of interest, purchase impulsively and then tell others what a wonderful experience we had. But that is the journey that many websites are set up for. Instead, most customer journeys are quite different, and more like the following:

▷ You realize you have a need for a product or service to solve a problem, simplify your life, perform a needed function, or simply provide entertainment, pleasure or security from potential losses.

▷ You then search online for brands that may have the products or services for the needs you seek to fill. You often search on Google or Bing with keywords or questions aligned with the need you seek to fill.

▷ You scroll down a list of search engine results until you find one that stands out. The first listings you will see will be the sponsored or paid listings. And then you'll see some that come up due to good organic SEO practices. Chances are you will stop on one that speaks to the function you are looking for to fill the need at hand. For example, I searched "outdoor winter gear" and got a varied list of results from backcountry gear to ski gear and clothing for people who work outdoors in cold places. The ones that stood out were the ones that spoke to a specific need: "Cold weather gear to keep you toasty all winter long," "Stay warm with best extreme cold weather gear," and "The best cold weather gear from people who work outside in the winter."

▷ You visit some of the sites in the search results that were served up to you. If you find what you are looking for immediately, you'll stay on one of those sites for a few seconds, maybe a minute or two to check out availability and price. If not, you will bounce by exiting or hitting the back button and going back to the search results that popped up earlier.

❯ You repeat the above with new search terms, and new browsing of additional sights until you find what fits your need or decide to abandon the process and go do something else.

Again, your website needs to be much more than another online store or sales pitch for services. It also needs to project a meaningful story that connects with your visitors and communicates clearly and concisely the value offered beyond a product.

Patagonia, one of the world's leading brands for building purpose and emotional connections with customers, does a good job of crafting stories on their website in which people wish to see themselves, just like we've been discussing throughout this book. Today, while writing this chapter just before the biggest gift-giving season of the year, their landing page engaged me with a message that was meaningful to who I am as a person (as well as millions of other people).

The first headline you see, overlaid on a video of people living out an adventurous story, is:

Gifts for a Good Story
Built for lifetimes of whatever brings them joy.

Who does not want to give a gift that brings a loved one a lifetime of joy? And who does not want to be part of a good story in their lives and those of others?

The next section, part of which you see before you need to scroll (which we've already established is key to getting people actually to scroll and stay on your site), is a block of customer categories. Women, men, kids, and so on, are followed by product categories—parkas, windbreakers, fleece, and so on—making it fast and easy to find what you are looking for before you have to start scrolling.

What follows next is the category that truly sets Patagonia apart from not just those in their category, but from most brands globally, period. This section is simply titled, Stories. The stories that follow are stories that matter to Patagonia's core customer groups. Stories featured during this visit of mine covered a 1,300-mile trek along the Pacific Coast Trail by a young family with three children under the age of 5; a letter from

Patagonia's president claiming that Earth is their only shareholder now; and another on why we humans keep buying stuff which focuses on the psychological aspects of reward that come from shopping and what this means for our environment and natural resources. The final sections present Patagonia's purpose.

Unless your purpose is to be the lowest price provider and sell mass quantities of fleeting products like Walmart or Target, you will succeed far faster if you build your website around the stories your customers want to see themselves in as related to your product category and share stories about the value of relationships with you, not just purchasing from you. Make it a point to keep monitoring websites of brands that do a good job of this, like Patagonia, to get inspiration for your own stories.

Let's go back to the pet grooming business. If this is your world, your website might feature stories about the joy you gave a dog, not just its humans. I had a poodle once, and every time she got groomed she would roam around the house with her head held high, prancing, and would often sit on the stairs waiting for me to take her photo, posing and looking straight into the camera like a fashion model when I did (yes, poodle brains are bigger than bird brains). Writing stories about how dogs came in matted or dirty, acting timid and then left prancing with a new pep in their step and sparkle in their eye are not just fun to read, they build trust for your services and enthusiasm for the joy you give dogs beyond a shampoo, haircut, and nail trim.

Before you start mapping out the sections you want in your navigation menu, think about your stories. Stories about the vision you have for your business, what inspired you to go on this journey of entrepreneurship, why you sell the products you do, what they mean for customers beyond the functional aspect of the products, and how you have built your business around creating an emotional value or fulfillment for customers. If you document these important elements, it will be much easier to build an engaging and persuasive website from the beginning.

Another step before you choose a website tool and start building out pages is to spend time reviewing sites of competitors, leaders in your industry, brands with whom you do business, and brands you tend to purchase from. Note the elements that help you find what you are looking for, elements that capture your attention, the personas, tones, and styles that keep you engaged and wanting to learn more. Examples of sites I believe do a good job of telling their brand stories, and making it easy for visitors to find what they need right away include Oracle.com, Godaddy.com, Apple.com, CharlottesWeb.com. There are many good websites out there. The more you browse the more ideas you will get for crafting a successful one of your own.

Enlighten and Inform

Keep in mind your website needs to inform, inspire, and enlighten visitors and give them reasons to come back and engage with your brand beyond your products. Those reasons could include:

> ❭ Tools that support the decision process such as mortgage or car loan calculators, total cost of tuition tools, and more.

> ❭ A library of industry reports, subject matter expert blogs, research reports, and more.

> ❭ UGC, user generated content, that shares real ideas from real people with other real people

> ❭ Compelling blogs that present new ideas, new product uses, technology updates, how-to guides, and so on.

As you discover what is most important to your customers, arrange the content according to what most influences decisions. On every page, layer copy elements in the inverted pyramid format which means the most important message you want visitors to leave with is at the top, then the second most important message, and so on.

Staying with the pet industry for the sake of example, if you are starting a pet boarding business, or doggy day care, you may want to consider including the following elements on your home page in the following order as they align with pet owners' priorities:

> ❭ Actual customer stories: Use testimonials about the wonderful care you provided your customers' canine children.

> ❭ Photos and videos that tell the stories of pets' experience in your care. Using visuals you take yourself instead of stock images better

tell the story of what you deliver. Use images of your staff interacting with happy dogs and even dogs interacting with each other. Pet owners want to see their pets happy, playing with new friends, and getting all the love and attention they typically get from their humans.

> ⟩ A list of distinct services you provide. If you take time to read books to dogs, give massages before bedtime, play a recording of their humans' voices to keep them assured they are coming back, and so on, make these elements visible when someone first lands on your page as they show a caring element others providers might not offer.

> ⟩ A succinct navigation menu. One of the first things anyone looks for when vetting out a new business to consider is price. Put a pricing tab on your menu so it's easy to find along with one that states your locations, hours of service, licenses, and so on.

> ⟩ Policy information. If you require reservations, make it easy to find information about cancellations and refunds. When it comes to our pets, it's hard to trust a provider you don't know and taking the fear out of making a reservation by offering a liberal cancellation policy will likely result in more reservations online.

Once you have determined the content you need to have on your website, create some design principles. What are the guiding principles for the development of your site that you will adhere to in order to assure relevance in words and design for visitors, and inspire them to stay longer.

Earlier I mentioned a statistic from a website viewing study conducted by the Nielsen Norman Group stating that 57 percent of time spent on a webpage is above the fold, or on the top half of a landing page. This is validation for the inverted pyramid approach to organizing your copy which leads first with what users are there to find and what will most influence them to dig deeper into your brand story and offerings.

A good process is to open up an Excel spreadsheet file and create a column for the home page, and another one for every tab in your navigation bar. In each column, list the content you need to include. For example, home page might include a slider to show the various elements of your pet boarding facility from the outdoor areas to the inside kennels and group playroom, followed by testimonials, a list of services, and information about locations and hours. Your About Us page column could have your business biography, achievements which you are most proud of, past positions held that add credibility to your business leadership skills, staff bios, and more. Another tab might be about Pricing for all your services. You may want to have another tab for Reservations, which would take people to a shopping cart where they could reserve space, order extra services like the massage and voice recording, shampoo, nail trim, special hair ribbons, and other services you offer. You could have a Testimonials page, but you can't count on visitors going to one. A better option would be to include at least one testimonial on each page.

Each element of your webpage should live in one section. You can include cross links to key sections such as the Reservations form on various pages for a simplified user experience, but you don't need to duplicate content.

Website Builders

Once you have a map of your website structure, and know which content you plan to put where, the next step is to select a website builder. The most popular options for easy-to-use DIY website builders include Wix, GoDaddy, Squarespace, Shopify, IONOS, and Web.com. It pays to look at review sites that list the features of each provider you are considering to get a side-by-side comparison, however, not all review sites are completely objective. Some list companies that pay to be listed vs. companies they have vetted out via research, customer surveys, user testing, and so on. Take the time to look for review sites that post reviews based on research, not payments, and read what customers say about the options that interest you. One that may be worthwhile is comparingwebsitebuilders.com, which does exactly what its name and URL says.

Key features and functions to look for in a DIY website builder include the following:

> ❭ Templates—Pre-built stylized pages that offer customization so that you can decrease design time while still creating a site that does not look exactly like everyone else's.

> ❭ AI facilitated design—You are a business owner, not a designer, and if you can use AI for design, it will save you a lot of time and likely

frustration finding the right elements, colors, designs, and layouts for a page people will want to stay on a while.

⟩ Blogging capabilities—These are key as blogs are essential to engagement, elevating your value as a partner, and your SEO.

⟩ SEO tools—Many website builders inherently include SEO tools and should be a must for any system you choose.

⟩ Website analytical tools—These will help you monitor impact and engagement of your key messages and individual pages quickly and in real time.

⟩ Video creation—If you don't have this feature in a website builder platform, you will have to get a subscription with a separate video builder platform which adds more cost, more time, and more systems to manage and track.

⟩ Online appointment scheduling—This is a tool that's important for B2B and service-based companies as it makes it easy for customers to book appointments with you.

⟩ Social selling tools—These tools will make it easier for you to integrate sales features in your social pages and use one system to manage and monitor these programs.

⟩ Domain specific email addresses—Some website providers provide you with an Outlook account for emails that align with your URL, letting you manage email addresses on your website dashboard.

⟩ Cart abandonment recovery—If you are running an e-commerce site, the cart abandonment feature will prompt potential customers to return to your site and complete their purchase if they navigate away.

⟩ E-commerce and payment systems—Most website builder tools have payment options for extra fees or within their premium packages. Find one that is not just easy for you to manage, but also easy for your customers to use and trust.

When you sit down to build your site, you will need to have a toolbox of brand assets ready to use to get you started. Assets include your images, original and stock, that reflect your story and products, your page text and content in final written form, reports, news features, and testimonials. Having these elements ready and organized in a file folder will make the work of building your site easier and faster. If you need stock images, and don't have a service that provides them, consider Adobe, Shutterfly, and Getty Images.

Setting Your Site Up for SEO and More

Building a website is not a one and done event in your marketing journey. You need to refresh it often. At the least you need to update your home page often so people feel like there is something new to learn when they come back. Elements of your site to update often include the hot topics listed on your home page, your news announcements, and your blogs. When you post blogs on social media pages and direct readers to your site to read the entire blog, the best way to get them to read beyond just the given blog page is to have new content easy to find. New content might include industry and business reports, news features about your brand, customer stories, and timely videos that showcase your product or tell a new element of your story.

Tagging is a big element of website maintenance and SEO. As search queries evolve and change for your category, so too should your site's meta and title tags. Tags are the terms or lists of keywords you put in your website's form fields for the site in general and for pages and images. Filling out these forms, or tagging your pages, helps SEO crawlers find you when web visitors are searching for given terms. Your website provides prompts for tagging your home page, each individual page, your blogs, content and images, making it easy to tag. Tag pages as you build them, and tag images as you upload them. You will need to update these tags frequently as you monitor query terms for your category. Browsing sites like Spyfu and SemRush will help you see which keywords are associated with your competitors so you can tag competitors' keywords on your website and compete for some of same visitors they are targeting. As you add more services, write more content, or expand into new markets, update your tags. Again, a big purpose of content marketing and blogging is to have content and assets you can tag to drive awareness for your site. Even if no one reads your content or blogs (not saying this is ideal), you will have the added value of SEO elements that can help you show up higher on search engine results pages.

You can enhance your SEO with plugins that are integrated into your website's content management system to help with SEO optimization and other functions.

Plugins for SEO help you optimize the impact of your meta descriptions and title tags throughout your site, and help you see how your keywords impact your SEO. Many plugins identify areas that need improvement and score your page's readability to help you keep people on each page longer. If you tend to be long-winded in your writing, you will likely get a yellow or red light for readability, and suggestions for editing your statements to be more concise and direct to the point. Yoast is one of the most established SEO plugins, originally built to just support WordPress sites, however it is expanding to other platforms as well. SemRush also provides SEO plugins to complement their keyword research tools allowing you to also manage competitor analysis, site audits, and backlink analysis with one system.

To sum it up, there is not a lot of point in spending time building a robust, interesting, dynamic, and engaging website if you are not going to put the effort in to drive your targets and customers to it. To do this, you need to develop, execute, and maintain strong SEO and Search Engine Marketing, which are not one and the same. Read on about this in Chapter 9.

GO TIME

Review competitor websites to identify their key messages and stand out promises and stories. Pay attention to the elements they include on their site and how they are organized to see if your content is as complete and easily organized for users to find quickly.

Determine your brand's stories and score them for relevance to customers, prospects, influencers, thought leaders, industry analysts, and other stakeholders you need to reach and influence. Summarize your most important stories in two to three paragraphs each, using the inverted pyramid approach to content organization.

Map out the content you need to have on your website. For example, pages for sections like About Us, Products, Pricing, Resources (News, Blogs), Case Studies, and Locations. Under each of these sections, list the specific pages you need to include to assure you include all the information your visitors will likely be looking for when landing on your page.

Make a list of the assets you need to tell your story on the home page and throughout your secondary pages. Again, the assets you need to gather include:

> Images including photographs and videos you have taken of your products or business, and stock images as needed.

> Infographics that lend credibility (and SEO as you tag these) to your story.

> Iconology that pulls your brand persona together (logos, graphics like swirls, dots, lines, and such that you use with your logo, your fonts, and other elements).

> Videos (15 seconds to 3 minutes) that you can use to pull people into your page and to provide how-to guidance and decision support.

> Content you will post and tag on your blog.

> News elements—press releases, features, mentions about your business that add credibility.

> Testimonials you have permission to use from customers.

Select a website builder and hosting company that fits your developmental needs and pricing. These sites offer templates with drag and drop simplicity, options for customizing templates or building your own site template if that is a skillset you have. Look for platforms that offer AI support for graphics, theme, and asset development to save time and money. As business and markets change quickly, its important to get an initial site up to introduce your brand in your markets as quickly as possible. You can always go back and change your design themes when you update your copy, content, and offers.

CHAPTER 9

Playing SEO and SEM Games without Losing Ground or Budget

Your messaging, content, and the marketing tactics defined in your plan are more likely to pay off if your brand has name recognition among your audiences. SEO programs are one of the main ways to get exposure as consumers use search engines for just about all information needs and decision assistance. Yet it's a myth that you have to pay a lot to be at the top of your category rankings. Instead, you just need to know how to execute campaigns, tag your website, and manage keywords for content and pay-per-click programs. And how to spy on your competitors' keyword usage.

This chapter will discuss:

⟩ Organic vs. Paid SEO and how to get started affordably and successfully with both

⟩ Investing time and resources wisely for PPC ads such as Google and Adroll

⟩ Managing keywords and hashtags to optimize Google Ads, retargeting clicks, and SEO

⟩ Keys to optimizing websites by tagging, blogging, and writing for SEO

⟩ Analyzing KPIs (Key Performance Indicators) for SEO

⟩ Monitoring competitive SEO data so you can affordably compete for rankings

EO and SEM are close, but not the same. SEO—search engine
optimization—refers to the organic actions you take to help your
website show up in search results. This includes tagging your site and
your pages, establishing back links, and tapping algorithms through cross
links, and so on. SEM—search engine marketing—refers to setting up paid
ads that put your website listing at the top of the SERP's (Search Engine
Results Pages) for Google, Bing, or other search platforms. Both SEO and
SEM rely on keywords, search query terms, tagging, and other common
actions to be successful.

Below are some important insights about both of these marketing
approaches and some tips to help you execute affordably.

SEO

Setting your website up for SEO is not complicated. It just takes an ongoing commitment to staying on top of your keywords, associated search
queries, site and page tagging, content development, and posting on various channels.

SEO is driven largely by organic efforts which include writing blogs
and other content that contain keywords aligned with your website, social
media pages, and other digital assets. The more your content gets clicked
on, shared, commented on, and viewed on your website the more they are
seen by the algorithms crawling through cyberspace. The more times these
algorithms become aware of your website and digital assets, the higher
your listings will show up on Google and Bing, and other search engines,
even if you do not have paid advertising accounts with these engines.
Following are some tactics to help you stay on top of SEO.

Keywords

You define your keywords by the words that represent what you do, the
value you deliver, and the terms your target audiences use when searching
for results in your category. For example, if you sell used automobiles in
Denver, Colorado, your keywords could include "used cars, used trucks,
quality used cars, luxury used cars, Denver," and the like. If you are

marketing software for insurance companies to better manage their customer retention, your words and phrases may include "insurance, insurance solutions, insurance business management, insurance marketing software, CRM for insurance brokers." Your keywords need to live on your website front facing pages and the backend programming side of it, such as the tagging form fields in your PPC (pay per click) advertising programs; and in the copy you use for all digital ads, social posts, assets, and content you push out to the worldwide web.

Query Terms

Search query terms are the terms that search engines identify as those most often used by web browsers looking for information or websites related to a given topic or category. People wanting to learn more about marketing consultants specializing in health care services may search, "health care marketing, marketing for physician practices, medical marketing agencies, healthcare marketing consultants in Tulsa," and so on. Search software such as that offered by SpyFu and Semrush provide glimpses of the terms and words most often used by people querying the web for information about given categories. They also provide insight into the keywords your competitors use to up their SEO results and show you which of the keywords you use are driving the most traffic to your website. You can access insights from these and similar sites for free or for a nominal monthly fee that will give you more access to data you can act upon.

Semrush, considered a gold standard in the industry as of this writing, provides in-depth insights about query terms resulting in traffic to your website and others in your industry, keywords, and backlinks associated with your website, search rankings, website domain authority, paid and organic search traffic to your website, and a lot more. It also allows you to compare your keywords and search results to your competitors. This and other SaaS platforms also list questions related to searches that showed your website listing and show you competitive links for paid and organic search outcomes.

Another popular source for SEO analysis currently is SpyFU. As its name suggestions, SpyFu is set up to let you spy on your competitors and does just this by showing you comparisons to other URLs you search, the common keywords and overlap for your site and competitors, and how much competitors in your space are paying and how much organic vs. paid traffic they generate with their SEO management. You will also get insights about backlinks referring the most traffic to your page, and your competitors' pages. This information is important for you to review as it will allow you to set your brand up for high SEO visibility and compete with other brands for awareness and web traffic, both of which are critical for new businesses.

SEO analysis platforms are important to help you understand where you stand in SEO ranking wars, how to outrank competitors, and what you might need to spend to do just that. Both tools I've mentioned, Semrush and Spyfu, are respected for helping you manage and compare your SEO effectiveness and competitiveness, although neither has a perfect reliability score. Use these tools and others like them to give you a good general understanding of the SEO landscape in your space and provide you with direction, but plan to get your actual and real time data by monitoring your own analytics, e.g., Google Analytics, regularly. There are other SEO analysis platforms you can choose from as well, and various price points for these services, including free access to limited insights. Take the time to find the right service for you

Tagging

Creating meta and title tags is a simple way to get noticed by algorithms and your target audiences as discussed in brief in Chapter 8. Tagging involves crafting short descriptions about your company on the backend of website pages and the Alt Text fields for images on your website. Fields for inserting your tags have limited characters so you need to spend time coming up with brief statements that contain keywords that set you apart, and appeal to browsers. Not always as simple as it may seem. These tags show up in search engine results pages, so take the time to really use your words wisely.

To nail the best terms for your tag fields, monitor the query terms for your industry regularly and update your website's tags accordingly to assure you are set up for the fickle changes in query terms and consumer behavior.

So, what is the difference in a meta tag and title tag? A meta tag is the description, often limited to about 155 characters, that tells search engines what your overall site is about. It is also the statement that appears under the heading of the search engine listing for your URL. This needs to appeal to browsers to get clicks. It may help with SEO rankings, but not as much as your title tag will. Your title tag is the tag you create for a webpage on your site. Semrush's guide to meta and title tags provides some good guidelines and examples for how to set these up. A current example they use is for recipes for peach cobbler. If you google websites for recipes you will get a list of websites with meta tags like "less stress more joy, recipes, how-to videos," and more which are the ones you will find for Simply Recipes and Allrecipes, two of the most popular sites for recipes for all types of food. If you search "peach cobbler recipes," you will see the title tag for the peach cobbler page on those sites. For example, on Allrecipes the title tag is "Fresh Southern Peach Recipe." When someone searches for the peach cobbler recipe, the associated page will show up under the URL name for Allrecipes, making the search results highly relevant for the browser. This example shows just how important it is to tag your pages with the keywords that are most likely to appeal to your audiences. You can also tag the images you use on each page. If you are a recipe site, you could tag the photo of that peach cobbler with keywords and competitive words like "award-winning recipe that competes with grandma's baking." Other sites use title tags like best, most popular, and so on to help their pages seem better than others.

As Google often changes the rules for how they align with meta and title tags, it is important for you to monitor these changes, adapt your website tagging strategies and terms, or find a programmer you can rely on to do it for you.

Backlinks

Earning backlinks for your website is quite a bit more complicated than inserting keywords into content and website back end prompts. Just as the first word of the last sentence says, you earn backlinks rather than simply set them up and monitor results. First, what is a backlink? A backlink occurs when a third-party site includes your URL. You can't just go through the web, find sites that relate to your business, and insert a back-link. You have to do something, or have something on your site, that the managers of those other websites want to reference and or include on their own. This is why it's important to build a marketing plan with messaging and content strategies that include educational and thought leadership elements. There are many ways to get backlinks for your site, some simple and some complex, but getting them is really critical for the visibility and credibility of your brand.

A backlink is like a recommendation or earned endorsement from a credible player in a field. For example, going back to peach cobbler recipes, if your recipe was featured on your local county fair's website in the form a link to your own website of recipes, you just got a backlink from a credible source in your local community. If you are in the robotics manufacturing business and your robotics firm just got featured as one of the most innovative companies for automated manufacturing on a media website, and that mention includes a live link to your URL, you just earned a really powerful backlink that tells Google's algorithms you are credible to media, which is a big endorsement. It also tells the algorithms that your website is worth showing in search results for related query terms.

There are many ways to earn backlinks for your website. You can pay to be listed in a category ranking on sites that provide Top 10 lists across business sectors, you can join associations and earn backlinks in member directories, you can submit your business URL and information to resource sites that are not pay to play, and you can do a lot of thought leadership activities to get media and others referencing your brand and URL.

Here are some actions that can help build credibility for your brand from third-party backlinks:

> Survey your customers about a hot current topic and post your findings on your website. Send a link to the page on your website to media, influencers, and others in your space and encourage them to include the link on their website and and social media pages.

> Send out press releases about your company's news. Product launches and new big client wins can be used to earn backlinks on frequently visited news sites. If you can get your clients to do joint

press releases with you and include live links in the press releases on their sites, you get an additional backlink and credible endorsement from a player in the industry.

〉 Add original interviews with industry leaders to your blog strategy. If you can interview third-party experts in your field and get them to include your blog posts on their site, you earn a backlink that adds credibility for algorithms, and for customers following the experts you include in your stories and blogs.

The above activities will help you earn highly valuable and credible organic SEO listings for which you do not pay. Organic scores help you show up just below the sponsored results on SERPs so it's important to keep up on organic activities such as those mentioned above and throughout this book. They are also more credible to searchers than paid ads as organic posts show an industry presence vs. a paid presence, and consumers are less and less likely to click on anything that is clearly an ad.

SEM

No surprise, Google is the leader for all things search, and Search Engine Marketing. And it is the most used platform for digital advertising. Google Ads, the global leader in its own universe for search engine marketing, allows anyone to create and publish ads that show up in search engine results for a given category. Currently Google represents 39 percent of the global digital marketing spend in 2023. For comparison, Facebook was in second at 18 percent and Amazon at 7 percent.

Getting Going with Google Ads

Like social media advertising on Meta and other channels, setting up and managing Google Ads campaigns is easy and flexible. You set the budget you are willing to spend, select your keywords, set up your ads, schedule and target audience, and then let Google's algorithms find the right search queries for showing your ads. Initially, Google Ads created simple search ads that consisted of a brand's keywords, a compelling message, and URL. Listings were ranked according to dominance of keywords and marketers stressed continuously over how to get listed on the first page of results and stay there. Now Google Ads allow you to do Search ads with images, aka display ads, and videos that use the power of YouTube. Quickly and easily. The rules of engagement for Google ads and SEM in general will continue to change as AI and other technology opens up new playing fields, rules, and new games altogether. Stay on top of these changes so you can stay on top of SEO rankings.

For now, to get started, you need a solid list of keywords that define your category and brand, products and distinct advantages, and search query terms that your targets use most often so you can show up when they search online. Google Ads platform will lead you through building headlines and body copy for your search ads. For example, you might be prompted to write three strong headlines and six or more body copy descriptions. All Google Ads are responsive, meaning they react to the search queries and deliver the most relevant message for the given searchers by mixing up your headlines with your descriptions and then serving those combinations to viewers according to the query terms used. Creating ads is easy, but getting at the top of the searches not so much, unless you are willing to outspend everyone else in your category locally or nationally or both. However, you can still be effective with a small budget depending how you set up your keyword lists, headline and descriptions, and geographical settings.

Here are some tips:

Optimize your keywords: Google allows you to set your keywords up for exact, phrase or broad match. Exact is just that. Phrase will show your results to searches that have a mixture of the words in a keyword phrase, and broad match will show your ads to searches with the words you choose and others that have similar meanings. For example, if you own a spa business, and use spa services as your keyword, a broad match that would pull up your ads could be massage, facials, and other services that are subsets of spa services. To optimize the number of chances your ads will show up, Google recommends setting your keywords to broad match with Smart Bidding. When you enable Smart Bidding, Google's machine learning tools automatically set bids for you according to the budget and goals you set, helping you increase performance and save time monitoring all your bids daily. If you choose phrase matching, your results will be more limited and choosing exact match means your ads will only be shown to queries that are exactly the same words in the same order as you typed them into your Google Ads dashboard. Exact match clearly narrows down the results.

Choose Your Assets: Including links to content on your website and images in your responsive search ads will help you show up more, be more noticeable, and ultimately get more clicks. Using videos in your ads will also enhance your chances of getting shown and noticed. Your goals should be to show up high in rankings and get clicks to your website.

Writing for Google Ads Algorithms: For responsive ads, you just need to write your headlines and descriptions copy using your keywords and the query terms you have identified for your audience. As you input your copy for ads and insert your URL links, Google will tell you the strength of your ad. With this instant Ad Strength monitor, you can keep editing until you achieve a high level of Ad strength which means your ads are more likely to show up to the right people at the right time. Google will guide you as you write, making suggestions for your headlines, your keywords, and whether or not you need more unique copy, and other tips that will strengthen your ads. This is one example of how AI can help optimize your efforts.

Use AI: Another option is to let Google's AI take over writing all your headlines and descriptions and serve them up according to automated Smart Bidding. It might be worth setting up one campaign with your own writing skills and another with Google's AI output so see which performs best. While you might be just as smart as the computers, you might also learn a few new tricks.

Managing the Bidding Wars

More than 80 percent of Google Ads advertisers use automated bidding, which suggests that anyone who does not has an immediate disadvantage. Manual bidding is hard to keep up with and since algorithms change so rapidly, as do the conditions and demographics associated with searches, it can be difficult to work at the pace automated bidding maintains. Smart bidding uses auction-time optimization and shows ads based on time of day, creative in ads, devices used for searches, a user's location, and more.

An example of how this feature works: Searchers in a city might get different ads than searchers in a rural area for the same query if their usage patterns and purchasing behavior differs. These differences are not just based upon providers near the searcher, but also on how city people use a product category differently than rural people do. The algorithms for your ads and search category learn from queries, not just your keywords, making them smarter than humans that don't know all the query terms computers see 24/7 from searchers around the globe.

Remember, you can set audience demographics per age, locations, interests, purchasing patterns, gender, and many other sorts so you only pay to be seen in areas in which you do business, and specific consumer categories to which you appeal the most, and which you have a higher likelihood of converting clicks to customers.

You determine the bid strategy you want to set up and pay for. Your strategy can be based on getting as many conversions as possible for your budget, achieving a target CPA (cost per action), or ROAS (return on advertising spend). Per Google, setting a ROAS goal is likely to produce more conversions than a CPA goal for a given amount of spend.

Setting a Google Ads Budget

Google charges users on a PPC model, which means you "pay per click" you receive for your ads. To reward advertisers and to optimize revenue streams, Google's search results first show ads that are sponsored, listings for which marketers paid more for the keywords shared by an industry than those who spent less. However, just because you paid for ads to appear in search listings does not mean your ads will show up on the top of a search page or before organic listings. If your budget per day or for keyword bidding is small, you may not be at the top of the sponsored search listings or above organic listings that have high algorithm recognition. A general rule is that anything less than $1,000 a month will not have much impact on your rankings. That can and most likely will change as the rules, processes, and algorithm for Google change frequently. And if you set your budget too low, your ads might not be shown enough to reach the budget you set. They have to show up to get clicked on. If your $500 set budget limit only results in $200 a month, it's not a good thing. Saving money means you likely missed out on rankings that could have helped you find new customers as you got outbid or out-purchased by others in your category. And it may mean you didn't get the click goal you set for your campaign.

Some Things about Google Ads to Keep in Mind

As noted just above, Google changes its processes, rules, and systems frequently, and machine learning and AI will continue to change how technology works for us and against us. Remember, Google Ads will show you your ads' strength scores, which ads and keywords perform the best for you, and which are not performing for your goals relating to impressions, clicks, and conversions. Visit your dashboard frequently to see how your ads are doing and if you are optimizing your budget with positive reach and conversion ratings.

Just like its bidding process, Google is smart in how they manage their clients. They schedule free consultations with you to help you optimize your ads, provide insights about what you can do to improve your creative, and of course tell you how you can get more by spending more. Your dashboard will provide an optimization score which you may be advised needs to be in the 90s, but this is not always relevant. In fact you can spend a lot of money to get a higher score which could easily not produce any more conversions for you. What you need to focus on is your conversions, not your clicks, as clicks could be from people you don't need to reach or they can be from bots which mimic human behavior on the web like clicking on URLs. If you get a lot of bots clicking on your ads, Google will likely credit your account back. The volume of bot "hits" you get is worth nothing as these are not human clicks you can convert to whatever your conversion metric might be.

The algorithms often show you what keywords to consider adding to your list. This can be a good thing and sometimes a not so good thing. Often the words are not optimal for your category and adding too many keywords to your account can actually dilute your performance. Instead of accepting all keyword suggestions, manually pick those that apply and ignore those that do not.

At the end of the day, money matters. You can read all the Google articles on how to optimize your account and results, but if you don't spend enough to compete with others in your space targeting your same locations, demographics, and so on, you simply won't show up as high on the search engine results pages. Ads—or rather listings—show up according to many factors, not just money spent. These factors include content aligned with keywords and search queries, how you craft the tags on your website, number and credibility of backlinks, and more as discussed previously.

Google Business Profile (formerly Google My Business): If you are a retailer this is an important tool to set up with Google. This is location-based marketing that will help you show up when people are shopping for what you offer. Searches on smart phones and computers for "coffee near me," "pizza near me," "urgent care near me," "bookstores near me" deliver options on Google maps, and when you click on one, a page about that brand comes up that most often provides their website link, phone number, hours, ratings, distance from searcher's location, and more to help searchers make quick decisions for purchases. As of this writing, setting up a Google Business Profile is free. If sparking impulsive sales, or sales among consumers traveling through your market area is key to your revenue stream, this is a must. To set up your Google Business Profile, you just fill out the forms on Google's program page, list all the key information about your business, and Google creates your page for you.

Retargeting

In simple terms, retargeting is another form of the PPC (pay-per-click) advertising. Retargeting platforms use browser-based cookies to show advertisements for your brand to visitors that left your website before completing a desired transaction or behavior. These platforms show past visitors ads about the products they viewed on your site, or about your brand in general, as they wander around the web on other sites. These ads are designed to remind visitors to purchase what they left in a shopping cart on your site, complete a Contact Us form to learn more, read a blog about making wise choices, and so on. Once you select a platform to use for retargeting, you place tags, or pixels, on your website so that the platform of choice can follow your visitors and inspire them to come back.

There are a variety of platforms you can use for your retargeting including, of course, Google. Google will enable you to place a Google tag on your website so that when someone leaves your page without completing a conversion action, e.g., making a purchase or completing a form, Google will follow them around to other Google properties like YouTube, Gmail, search results pages, and show them an ad to remind them to go back to your site and further engage. Important to note is that Google only retargets to Google properties, which can limit your retargeting reach and the potential learnings from this critical form of marketing.

Another platform to consider is AdRoll, a popular retargeting platform that follows visitors to multiple sites vs. those belonging to a single enterprise. If you need to reach customers on more than Google and YouTube and Gmail, you will want to set up a third-party retargeting account that follows your audiences across multiple channels. AdRoll and other services like it work a lot like Google does. You set up custom ads for display and retargeting, using your creative in their templates, and sort audiences within the parameters they set up for you. AdRoll then integrates with a wide net of publishers to maximize your reach to past visitors to your site, new customers, and lookalike audiences, which look like your visitors and customers, that you can set up on your account. Your ads can appear across popular social channels including Facebook, Instagram, LinkedIn, Google Ads, and many others.

There are many reasons retargeting is important. Just one is that the platforms used will show you the websites where your visitors went after visiting your site so you can get a glimpse into what interests them, where they may lean politically, and the entertainment they seek. Knowing this information can inform your ad tone and purchases as you set up digital ads across third-party sites and help you build accurate personas of your target audiences and relevant messaging.

Other reasons retargeting matters is summed up in a blog posted by Spiralytics in October 2023. Some of these reasons include:

- ▶ 400 percent increase in engagement rates (Vibe.co)

- ▶ 1,046 percent increase in searches for a brand name associated with retargeting campaigns (Connectio and PR Newswire)

- ▶ 10 times higher Click-Through Rates (CTR) for retargeted ads over typical display ads (AdRoll)

- ▶ 70 percent higher likelihood to convert for retargeted users (SharpSpring)

GO TIME

Map out the activities you need to set up and maintain for organic SEO. These include tagging, blogging, use of keywords throughout your site, establishing backlinks with related businesses, media, and more.

Set up a Google Ads account and a Google Business Profile account and start populating your keywords, audience sorts, and business parameters.

Select a retargeting platform you can use affordably for the long-term if your CRM or other marketing technology platforms do not offer this service. Set up your ads according to your goals, and monitor the engagement, clicks, and websites visited frequently to learn more about what interests your visitors, and what type of messaging will get them to come back and complete a call to action or transaction abandoned on your website.

Monitor all activity regularly to see where your time and money is paying off the most, which keywords, responsive ad headlines and body copy, display images and messages, or incentives drive the best performance. All of these ad platforms discussed allow you to make budget and ad changes instantly, pause ads, or cancel at any time so that you can stop ads that are not working and put more money behind those that are.

Set your goals for display ads, Google Ads, and retargeting so you don't waste time and money setting up programs. Be realistic according to your budget and time to set up, manage, and monitor these programs.

CHAPTER 10

Thought Leadership as a Marketing Strategy

We humans are wired to follow winners not losers, authorities not novices. And more and more, not to respond to ads as much as we respond to the advice or insights shared with us by people we trust in government, news, business, entertainment, and more. This is an aspect of human nature that has not and is not going to change anytime soon. In addition to building your brand's presence in your category online and within your market communities, you need to position yourself, and/or your team members as authorities in your field.

This chapter will walk you through:

▷ The process and power of taking a stand for something that is much larger than your brand

▷ Why thought leadership about societal and business issues matter

▷ Formats and channels for establishing your authority

▷ Tips for starting a thought leadership program

With the majority of consumers reporting they find ads more and more annoying, it's important to communicate with authority not just advertising dollars. Thought leadership programs are a highly effective way to do just this.

Thought leadership is a powerful approach to marketing any brand, especially in the B2B, industrial, and technology spaces and for high-risk, complex consumer purchases. While it usually takes longer to see a direct impact on revenue, this strategy is essential to setting up your business for awareness, credibility, partnerships, and sustainable growth as a market leader and subject matter expert.

Understanding Thought Leadership

So, what actually is Thought Leadership? Thought leadership is about serving as a source for subject matter expertise in your business category, with subject matter experts (SME) defined as those that have in-depth knowledge about a given industry, field, or topic which was accumulated by experience, professional achievements, education, licenses, and so on. And then using your position as a SME to lead the narrative about new thoughts, ideas, and innovations within your field. This is often achieved by sharing opinions not just facts, inspiring new ideas and innovations throughout an industry, and addressing current issues with actionable insights others can benefit from practicing.

As an entrepreneur in the business category you have chosen, chances are you are already a subject matter expert due to your expertise and prior accomplishments. You don't need to be a household name in your field or even the most successful business operator in your market. You just need to know your business, be up to date on the issues facing your industry, under-stand the fears and anticipations that hold true for your target customers, and develop your position and voice. Once you determine your voice, and your position on key issues, there are many methods for communicating and many channels for getting heard. Methods and channels for thought leadership marketing are very similar to those used for PR campaigns.

Restating what people already know or can find elsewhere is not thought leadership. Daring to say what others have not, taking a stand on something that matters to society not just you, even sparking controversies to get important national narratives started are examples of thought leadership, and the kinds that build awareness for a brand, its values, its leaders, and its character. Brands, like people, who choose to stand for something other than falling for anything are the ones that most often emerge as leaders worth following.

Standing for Something That Matters beyond Your Business

One aspect of thought leadership is to take a stand on issues that may not be popular, and could even be risky, but leaders dare to do so anyway.

Remember Colin Kaepernick, the NFL player who lost his career when he chose to protest police brutality by kneeling during the national anthem? Although he continued to state his position was not against the military, many media players and political influencers like the 45th president of the U.S. jumped on it and called him out for being anti-American and a disgrace to the NFL. Even with many others in the NFL joining him in kneeling against police brutality, he was the only one to entirely lose his career options as a result. Eventually, Roger Goodell, the NFL commissioner, apologized to Kaepernick for not listening to his real reason for kneeling, but long after irreversible damage was done to his reputation, which made him "untouchable" as a quarterback, as no team wanted to direct the anger toward him to their team. My point in bringing this up is not to restir the angst Kaepernick's silent protest caused, but to show the impact taking a stand can have on brands.

In 2018, nearly two years after Kaepernick started protesting against police brutality, Nike created an ad called, "Dream Crazy." It featured athletes doing what seemed to be the impossible. The ad ended with Kaepernick walking toward the camera saying, "Don't ask if your dreams are crazy, ask if they are crazy enough." This ad campaign became global news not just for its message, "Believe in something even if it means sacrificing everything," but because it tied Nike to the controversy associated with Kaepernick's protest against police brutality. There was immediate backlash. People posted videos of them burning their Nike shoes, the then

President of the United States escalated the issue by calling for people to fire any NFL player that did the same and calling him unpatriotic, despite it becoming clear that the protest was not against military or patriotism for the US, but police brutality. Media, politicians, and every day people escalated this into one of the biggest controversies of the time.

The immediate fallout from the Nike ad was a stock decline of about 3 percent. But then celebrities and others started to see the protest for what it was, and started speaking out against police brutality, and buying and wearing Nike shoes in public appearances to show support for change. NFL owners locked arms together with their players before the National Anthem at games, showing support for their team's position on police brutality. Nike's stock soared to an all-time high, and sales went up 31 percent in addition to the ad breaking records for social media posts and media coverage. In the end, the media value earned was $163 million and the brand value generated was $6 billion, becoming one of the greatest public relations moves of any brand, not just Nike.

Let me back up. I am not suggesting you start a protest, or seek out controversy for the wrong reasons, one of which is to achieve monetary gain versus positive social change. I am suggesting you go back to the values you outlined in Chapter 1 and build on the issues for which it is important you take a stand. Are you in an industry that minimizes minorities, women, or others? Exploits the earth's resources for a few? While these may not be a direct result of your business, they might be associated with your industry and if so, you can promote your values for change and show what you are doing to minimize the impact you make by being in the industry. By starting a business around a cause like some of the brands mentioned throughout this book, your chances of being heard as a thought leader are higher, and when that happens your brand gets mentions and people start paying attention. When consumers associate brands with their own values, they are more likely to buy, as pointed out by research referenced in earlier chapters. It is really hard, and often too expensive, to get your brand national recognition quickly. Being part of a solution needed in your community or industry and gaining attention as a thought leader worth following will help you get known for good without spending a fortune on ads to just simply get your name out there.

Businesses can further critical societal solutions in many ways as a thought leader proposing change in industries related to their products. Some of the ways that matter most to purchasers include reducing carbon footprints, furthering fair trade and labor practices, reducing poverty and hunger, fundraising for medical research, and more. Taking a stand can manifest in many ways as well. For example, posting your positions on your website and social media pages, participating in local fundraisers, volunteering to support local charities or programs, donating proceeds to organizations that serve others, and the like. Patagonia has participated in many programs to help with climate change. In 2011, they took their position a step further and ran a Black Friday ad in the *New York Times* that featured one of their jackets and the headline, "Don't buy this jacket." The ad encouraged consumers to consider their impact on our world through potentially unnecessary purchases that may seem innocent, but actually add to the substantial drain on resources, increase pollution, and add to harsh labor practices in challenged economies. The purpose of this headline was to get people thinking about repairing what they have and reusing instead of always buying new when that was not always necessary. The idea was that if your zipper is broken, the jacket is not a total loss. Let Patagonia fix the zipper and lower your consumer imprint. Interestingly, the ad increased sales by 30 percent. And it wasn't because of the fashion appeal of the black and white image of a plain fleece jacket. It was because people want to follow leaders whose values they believe in. Patagonia' customers believe in protecting the environment and this add sang their song.

Ads like the two mentioned above for Nike and Patagonia clearly show creative presentation of thought leadership which helps to garner widespread attention and viewership. Both achieved such an impact that they also propelled media coverage, social media comments and posts, and other thought-provoking public discussions about the ads, which added to the public discussions about the issues, the brand, and positively impacted sales and stock values. While gaining revenue should not be your goal, it can often be a byproduct of doing good, which is a good thing for any business.

Why Thought Leadership Matters

It goes without saying that consumers don't respond to ads nearly as much as they respond to informative, insightful, and inspirational content. And when that content strikes a chord, they are likely to follow the brand associated with the thought leader behind the message, and consider that brand for purchases and/or partnerships.

There are many ways you can build a thought leadership position for you and your brand. Whatever direction you take, its important you build out a plan around a position you are willing to promote, stand behind, live consistently around per your brand actions and values. It won't always be easy. But in most cases, when executed accurately, it will be worthwhile.

If you decide to build and execute a thought leadership plan, note the various ways consumers and purchasers digest thought leadership marketing according to a report by iResearch Services:

> Digital content   59 percent

> Online events   49 percent

> Social media   34 percent

> In-person events   33 percent

> Print   28 percent

Given the strong numbers above, your thought leadership marketing plan should cover most if not all of the above formats. It also needs to cover the tone of thought leadership that consumers of it seek. This same report by iResearch Services shows that 46 percent of consumers of thought leadership content say most of what they read is too salesy; and 40 percent say in most cases the content does not share any new ideas. Additionally, 64 percent want a more human tone vs. a sterile corporate tone, and that they value content written by an individual vs. a brand. LinkedIn reports that more than 50 percent of those surveyed said they read thought leadership content, but 71 percent say more than 50 percent of the material they read is not valuable to them. This is key, because it means if your content is valuable, providing something new and/or actionable, yours will get read while many of your competitors' content might not.

Building Your Thought Leadership Plan

To start, it's important to note the difference in thought leadership content and content for content marketing as discussed in Chapter 6. Thought leadership is meant to evoke thoughts, conversations, and actions while other content is often designed to start sales conversations, provide decision support, and/or generate new transactions. Again, while consumers tend to engage with content they find thought-provoking or game-changing, they also tend to form bonds with and trust for the leader behind the message and are more likely to purchase from that brand. Some steps to thought leadership follow.

Secure Your Thoughts

The first step in developing a thought leadership marketing plan is to identify themes for which you can credibly emerge as a SME and thought leader. Keep in mind the themes you write about need to be current, of direct relevance to your market, and ones for which you can present new ideas and insights. Topics currently at the top of many businesses leaders minds include staffing and DEI issues, sustainability and ESG issues, responsible capitalism, responsible resourcing, fair labor practices, CSR, adapting to AI and the pending changes to the workforce, manufacturing processes, supply chains, and so much more. Focus on topics for which you and your team are experts that are of current relevance to the markets you serve.

Establish Your Targets

Define the audiences that can gain the most from your insights or opinion and are most likely to engage with you as a result of your position. What topics matter most to those audiences? Do you need to build thought leadership content for diverse customer segments? If so, how do you need to adapt your themes, messaging, tone, and channel strategies?

Build Your Talking Points

Once you decide on the themes around which you want to emerge as a thought leader, the next step is to outline three to five key points on each theme that are important to communicate, and for which you can provide new insights, ideas, or strategies. Keep these points objective, insightful about the industry not your brand, and actionable when possible for your readers.

Look for valid research studies that back up any claims or challenges you make so you can add credibility for any truths you choose to share or myths you want to dispute. Adding data to back up your position just adds credibility to your theme and shows responsible thought leadership instead of hyped-up rhetoric.

Decide on the Channels of Delivery

List the channels most used by the audiences you identified as most important to reach and most likely influenced by your thoughts. What channels do they use most for news, professional or industry information, and decision support for making purchases? Your channels might include media outlets, podcasts, talk and news radio stations, cable TV, newsletters for local and national business organizations, in addition to social media, email, text, and so on.

Now list the specific outlets within the channel categories you listed above that are appropriate for delivering your message. If you listed radio talk shows, you might consider your local National Public Radio affiliate and talk shows. Newsletters might include those put out by chambers of commerce, national associations, etc.

With all of the above, it's time to start preparing your content. Instead of writing your story in academic or corporate language, use your individual voice, and be bold, daring, and most importantly confident. A good formula for composing thought leadership content includes:

- ❯ Stake out a position on an issue, event, or current affair that matters beyond your brand.
- ❯ Clearly state the problem and how your position reflects a solution that benefits many.
- ❯ Back up your position with verifiable data.
- ❯ Explain your position.
- ❯ Defend your position against opposing viewpoints.

Going back to the research listed earlier, consumers will engage longer with content written by an individual not a company. If it reads like its written by your PR team or firm, it loses the human touch which elevates the ability to create an emotional response. Not a strong persuasive writer? Try asking your AI app to give you a foundation upon which you can edit to add more facts and emotional appeal, or hire a writer on a contract basis.

Remember, your thought leadership material does not need to be a dissertation or any kind of long, detailed production. It just needs to be a statement on a position backed up by facts and presented with the kind of persuasion that aligns others with your opinion. A successful approach to writing content is to be firm in your position and opinion, clear about your statements and purpose, and convincing in order to get others to believe in your thinking and share your content with their own networks. Having verifiable data to back up your positions and examples is critical as well.

Once you have drafted content, you can parse it to fit various formats. For example, craft a summary for social media posts, adapt it for a press release, feature story pitches to editors, guest column for an industry publication, and more.

Leading with Thoughts across Channels

Here are some considerations for getting out there on various social media channels.

LinkedIn

If you are in the B2B world and want to become a thought leader among executives of companies you want to do business with, LinkedIn is your stage. Keep in mind it is also the stage for about 900 million others who want their thoughts and ideas read around the world, too. Even if you are a new player in your industry, and are just starting your first business, you can still break out on LinkedIn. It takes time, but this channel can pay off in many ways. The key is to get started and stick with it.

Here are some tips:

Post Frequently—Instead of posting all your thoughts and opinions about a given topic all at once, pick highlights from your position statement and organize it into a series of posts. Keep your posts short, direct, and speak with your passion, not just your intellect. Short is key per a new acronym people are using to comment about content posted—TLDR—which stands for Too Long Didn't Read. Passionate, powerful, and to the point tends to work best for getting noticed, read, commented on, and shared. All of which are important to establishing yourself among your network and others' networks. If your expertise is organizational management, post frequently about the hot topics on the minds of business managers, like the impact AI is having on hiring and operations and production. What are some of the realities relating to DEI (Diversity, Equity, Inclusion), remote work, and so on. Be bold and ask for comments.

Spark Comments—As mentioned before, to get noticed by the LinkedIn algorithms that search for posts and show them to people interested in given topics on LinkedIn, you need comments, likes, and shares. The more comments you get, the more the algorithms see you as someone whose voice matters to many, and so your posts get served up to the pages of others beyond your network.

To get comments, ask for them. Make a statement or pose a question aligned with your position and ask others if they agree, disagree, or have a completely alternative point of view. When someone comments, comment back. Doing so sparks more conversation and more algorithms.

Use Hashtags—Use hashtags in all your posts. These are the words you put behind hashmarks, like #thoughtleader. When you input these at the end of your post, LinkedIn will often show you the current search volume for that term or phrase. Be sure to include related terms that show up a lot. This means when people go to the LinkedIn search bar, and search that term, your post has a decent chance of showing up.

To gain respect as a thought leader on LinkedIn, you need to gain a lot of followers. Having a lot of followers, and therefore a lot of likes for your posts, helps you get noticed and read. You can gain followers by inviting people on LinkedIn to accept a connection with you, and by participating in LinkedIn Groups. Joining a group allows you to post to people you have not yet connected with and start conversations on topics related to the group. Many groups have thousands of followers, and enable you to expand your network quickly.

Again, creating a group is another way to get noticed as a thought leader. Set up a group around a given topic and invite people to join you there to discuss topics of mutual interest. You manage the posts, set the

tone and start discussions, giving you control of the narrative and exposure as a leader on the topic at hand.

Once you start building a presence on LinkedIn and start some
interesting discussions, send the links to your posts to your customers
and prospects in email campaigns, post them on other social pages, like
Facebook, to help you engage as many others as possible.

Keep in mind that videos do well on LinkedIn, not just written statements. You can make a video on your computer of yourself speaking your
opinion and calling for support among your peers, and post it very easily.
Short videos on LinkedIn do best so craft your talking points carefully.

LinkedIn allows you to set up short polls on your page which can
get a lot of attention. Posting polls about a topic related to your thought
leadership position can get people thinking about a given topic, and more
likely to follow your page or reach out for more information. People like
to answer polls to see how much they think like their peers. For example,
asking a question like "Which marketing channel do you plan to use the
most this year?" will make many wonder if their plan is aligned with others
plans so they will take your poll to get access to others' answers. Polls can
help you get validation for your position and data you can share in your
narratives to add credibility to what you have to say.

Podcasts

As an entrepreneur, you may be hard pressed to find the time to start
a podcast and keep it going regularly enough to make it worthwhile.
However, you can be a guest on others' podcasts and get a lot of mileage
for your leadership position. Take some time to explore podcasts on your
topic and make a list of those that have the most listeners per episode and
followers in general. Note the type of topics they cover and the guests they
have had. When you find some that seem to be a good fit for your topic
and position, reach out to the hosts and ask about participating in a future
episode. They are always looking for topics and guests and likely will at
least consider your proposal. If you have established a voice on LinkedIn,
and have built up a nice network of followers, 3,000 plus connections, you
will have a better chance of getting their attention and getting an interview.

Conference Presentations

One of the best ways to emerge as a thought leader is to speak at industry events. If you have a strong topic, a new point of view, an innovative idea to share, it is not as hard as you might think to become a sought-after speaker. The key is to come up with a catchy title and a compelling session description and submit applications to conference coordinators. Visit the websites of the associations in your field often, get a date for RFPs, deadlines, and submit proposals to as many that make sense for your position of expertise. Speaking at events as a SME for an association that is respected in your field makes you an automatic thought leader. Make a point to promote all of your presentations on all your social media pages, on your website, and via customer and prospect emails to build instant credibility for a very low cost. Try to film at least part of your sessions so you can show other event planners your speaking style and abilities, and again use short video snippets for social media posts.

Media Mentions

You don't need an expensive public relations agency to get mentioned in the news. You just need to put together a list of media editors and reporters covering your industry for local, national, and industry publications, and reach out with news that is meaningful to their readership. Put together a story pitch which is simply an outline of a topic that is current, why it matters to readers, and what readers will learn that will change how they do what they do for the better. Build your pitch around your thought leadership position, add some data to validate your position, and email to editors and reporters, podcast hosts, and others curating stories for public distribution. You should also consider pursuing guest column opportunities for local and trade newspapers and websites.

GO TIME

Decide on a topic for which you are a SME and can build a thought-provoking position around.

Craft some content around your position and start pushing it out across social media, your email platforms, and website.

Identify podcasts and conferences that cover your industry and are good fits for your message and position. Craft interview pitches, complete request for proposals, and start lining up interviews and speaking engagements.

Monitor feedback for your position, positive and negative, and increases in followers, likes, comments and shares, to determine which appeals, messages, and channels get the most attention for your position and leadership.

Keep thinking. Keep expanding on your position by referencing research, data, case studies, examples, and other third-party validation, and add updates, new evidence, and more to your presentation of your position as available. And build on new ideas and opinions. Keep new and original thoughts coming, and when possible do some of your own, original research, consumer polls and surveys, and use the findings to showcase information and insights you have about questions others may not know to ask.

Remember, thought leaders don't just have inspirational and game-changing ideas to share, they are rooted in integrity, transparency, and truth. If you don't live by these virtues in your business practices, no one will believe anything you say or do.

CHAPTER 11

Selling Strategies and Tactics That Turn Leads into Revenue

You are a business of one, or maybe five to ten. That's a great start, but the most likely the reality is you're on a slow, and cluttered road to catch up with established brands. While you may not be able to hire many marketing and sales staff yet, you can build leads and sales by building networks of partners, resellers, and affiliates. This chapter presents a few approaches to consider about building sales and scaling quickly while increasing the value of the customers you have, the fastest pace to sustainable growth. Here are a few of the topics covered:

> Selling to the Decision Process

> Partnerships

> Resellers

> Account Based Marketing

> Mapping Out Decision Journeys

company I once worked with put thousands of dollars into marketing programs to showcase their brand, from a six-figure trade show booth, generous Google Ads, retargeting and promotional budgets, to event sponsorships, and more. And even though they generated leads, they gained little to nothing in sales revenue for one simple reason. They had no sales strategy and no plan for nurturing leads on a meaningful journey to conversion. Needless to say, this business did not take off. And needful to say, just because you build a business, execute frequent and varied marketing campaigns, sales won't simply come in on their own. You can't ignore the critical extension of all things marketing: *selling*.

No matter what business you are in, B2B or B2C, selling is hard. Leads you generate don't always morph into sales, and sales do not automatically transform into repeat and loyal customers. You have heard it before. You need to invest in relationships that provide value beyond expectations in order to maintain revenue beyond initial sales. This holds true for both B2B and B2C brands. Regardless of what you sell, you need to establish trust for customer advocacy, services, and your commitment to follow through on the promises you made to get someone to even talk about doing business with you. It is not an overnight process, especially if your business involves more complex purchases than choosing a food truck in the park on a sunny Saturday afternoon.

Many entrepreneurs, unwittingly, jump out of the starting gate and make the same mistake many struggling existing businesses have made and will continue to make—develop sales messaging and processes around their mindset, not the mindset of their customer. The mindset of customers across any category with a slightly complex decision process is to invest in the processes that will set them up to make wise informed decisions, not ones they will regret. And because of prior experiences that did not work out as planned, and a general lack of trust among businesses in many categories, many prospects going into a sales cycle are looking for reasons why they can't trust a brand more than why they should. It's where society is stuck right now.

Appealing to the Decision Process

Decision processes are increasingly complex, but still rooted in age-old decision journeys. Below is an example of a decision journey for a B2B purchaser.

1. Decide there is a problem to solve or a need to fill.
2. Look for solutions to solve the problem to fill that need.
3. Research supplier options for products and/or services that can help reach goals.
4. Search for companies that offer selected options.
5. Select companies to consider and compare reputations using online review sites.
6. Identify companies to contact and visit websites to assess offerings, promises, pricing, and more.
7. Fill out a Contact Us or Sales Demo request form.
8. Schedule product demos with selected suppliers.
9. Review proposals.
10. Assign business to a selected provider.
11. Install, implement, and/or start using the product or service.
12. Assess satisfaction with product and brand's responsiveness and service.
13. Repeat purchase, assign loyalty, and refer others.
14. Switch to another brand.

For consumer retail journeys, the steps change when you get to the Contact Us forms for scheduling a demo. A retail consumer purchasing something that is not complex like a car, but simpler, like weight loss pills or a sweater, will make a purchase and go from Step 5 to Step 10.

Many entrepreneurs and sales leaders are not patient enough to align with a multi-step process and just push for a fast sale at every opportunity they find. A good example is what I've seen recently in higher education.

Universities will post social media ads about degrees they hope are of interest to prospective students. As soon as someone clicks on an ad they are taken to a landing page that has a visual and then a huge sales, "apply now" form that takes up a large part of the landing screen, above the fold. Little to nothing more about what the university or a specific program can do for individual learners. This is problematic in many ways.

Choosing a college is not a simple decision like ordering pizza for Monday Night Football. A pizza company with a coupon on a landing page that is "in the face" of users is likely going to convert. However, a university that is trying to get applications from learners vetting them and others is not. Students, their parents, and other influencers spend a lot of time researching universities before spending money and time to apply. They want to know who the leaders are, what their core competencies are, see a list of courses to see how current, rigorous, and inspiring their programs are, and they want to see job placement records for the degree areas in which they are interested in pursuing. Simply seeing a small Facebook, Instagram, or YouTube ad that says, "Get a degree and pursue a career in this cool field" is not enough to many qualified prospects to commit to the time it takes to fill out a form that takes over your landing page, or to give you their personal contact information so your call center can call them night and day until you give up or they choose to block your from reaching them. But this is what many universities and other brands do, because they are hyperfocused on filling recruitment quotas quickly while their best prospects are hyperfocused on taking their time to make the right decision.

Lesson learned here: Nurture customers along their purchasing journey, not your sales quota racetrack.

Going back to the 14 steps, here's an example of what your sales journey should look like from the lens of your targets if you want to convert qualified leads. Let's assume your category is building automation systems for manufacturing, a category you've learned by now fascinates me. Here's how you could address the steps of the above decision process in ways that directly align with the mindset of the purchaser.

Step 1: Decide there is a problem to solve or a need to fill.

> ❯ Leaders of manufacturing operations have a need to produce products faster while lowering the cost per unit and reducing waste.

❯ Possible responses:

- *Associate your brand with your track record for accelerating time to market, lowering products costs, and manufacturing waste all of which contribute to a high ROI.*
- *Where there is a tangible problem to solve there is often an emotional void to fill. Helping manufacturing directors optimize production ROI provides security, confidence, pride, and a sense of self-actualization.*
- *Craft your brand positioning statement and key messages that quickly show your ability to solve the problem at hand. Put these statements front and center on all your marketing assets to help your brand be known for precisely what customers need.*

Step 2: Look for solutions to solve the problem or fill that need.

❯ Operations managers look at various methodologies that can optimize their production efficiency: automation systems, robotics, assembly and inventory management, and more.

- *Craft key messaging about your businesses' distinct systems and quantifiably show the improved outcomes customers experience with your products, intellectual goods, and services.*
- *Integrate these messages throughout all your communications and marketing assets: ads, emails, social posts, trade show collateral, sales presentations, and proposals.*

Step 3: Research options for products and/or services that can help you reach goals.

❯ Purchasers do a lot of research to help them make the right decision as a bad decision can have pretty serious professional and personal consequences, and often have a list of criteria suppliers need to meet to be considered.

- *Talk to customers and survey prospects to identify what the decision criteria is for the customers you want to close. Communicate how you meet criteria for the ones you meet, and then find ways to improve in the areas in which you fall short. Communicate your qualifications to be the purchaser's final choice via personalized emails and sales presentations.*

Step 4: Search for companies that offer selected options.

❯ Purchasers across all industries use search, primarily Google, to find options. They go to review sites to see which companies are most popular and highly reviewed, and they visit websites of the brands that stand out during their research.

- *You can't communicate the value you bring per the solutions sought if no one knows about you. This is where your content marketing strategy and SEO plans become critical.*
- *Create Google Ads using responsive headlines and ad descriptions that cater directly to the criteria and qualifications customers seek in their decision journeys.*
- *Create content for your website and social pages accordingly so you show up higher on SERPs with the right messaging.*

Step 5: Select companies to consider and compare reputations using online review tools. Consumers pay attention to what others are saying about the brands they are considering and even one bad customer comment or a few low ratings can take you off the short list.

- *Monitor your brand reputation by first taking ownership of your page on sites like Yelp and Google Profile and responding to both negative and positive comments.*
- *Ask happy customers to post reviews about you on third-party sites and help you stand out for the quality you deliver.*
- *Collect testimonials and use cases to share with prospects in sales proposals, at trade shows, and throughout your website.*

Step 6: Identify companies to contact and visit websites to assess offerings, promises, pricing, and more.

❯ Once purchasers have a short list they will go to websites to learn more.

- *It is important you have your key messages and distinctions front and center and make it easy to find other information critical to decision processes, which includes information*

about the people behind a brand, the vision, the financial via-
bility, pricing, and so on.

- *People buy from people so communicate your qualifications*
  and those of your team to reach your business goals, your com-
  pany's record for success, financial backers, and so on.
- *Show your successes and stability. Experienced people and*
  stable finances matter, as no one wants to invest with a manu-
  facturing partner that might not be operating in a year, forcing
  them to start a long and complex decision process again, cost-
  ing valuable time and money.

Step 7: Fill out a Contact Us or Sales Demo request form.

〉 Purchasers who find what they need on a company's website will
often complete a Contact Us form to get answers to questions and
set up a call with a sales rep.

- *Make it easy for people to find your contact or sales demo*
  forms from any page they are viewing.
- *Keep forms simple and fast to complete and only ask questions*
  you need to, omitting any that seem too personal.
- *Follow up immediately to book a time. If your competitors*
  get that sales meeting first, you could be playing catch up to a
  similar company that proved themselves to be more responsive
  than you.

Step 8: Schedule product demos with selected suppliers.

〉 Purchasers want an introduction to the companies that have made it
on their short list and want time to ask questions to see if products
and brands are a good fit.

- *It's tempting to make this first conversation your biggest sales*
  pitch, but that usually does not go well. Learn to listen, answer
  questions you can, document questions you can't and use them
  for a reason to follow up with a personal email or proposal.
- *After an initial conversation or email exchange, you now have*
  permission to contact the interested consumer and start a con-
  versation about their needs. Follow up with messages about
  how you can help them instead of a sales pitch.

- *Keep the first meeting and conversation with you about them, not you. Once you show your ability to deliver on solutions needed and willingness to be a partner before a vendor, you will likely have many future opportunities to sell yourself.*

Step 9: Review proposals.

❯ Customers may provide companies on their short list with an RFP (request for proposal) so they can compare all providers equally and based upon the same criteria. Or, they may simply ask for a quote and scope of work statement from you.

- *A big mistake many companies make is to do a demo and end it without asking a really important question. "May I send you a proposal and scope of work to show you what we can do for you per the goals you need to achieve?" You need to make it routine to ask if you can send a proposal.*
- *If your proposal is impressive enough and meets all their criteria, you could force an early decision in your favor. If they say no, there is no harm done to you. So ask!*

Step 10: Assign business to a selected provider.

❯ Purchasers go through a long process and make the most informed decision they can as a result of the information gathered and experiences with brands vetted.

- *Providing prospects with objective decision guides like checklists can help them make wise decisions while positioning you as a partner that helps them do what is best for them, not always you.*
- *When you send a proposal, include information on what to look for in partners and suppliers in your category as appropriate. Keep this checklist objective and add some testimonials at the end.*

Step 11: Install, implement, and start using the product or service.

❯ Once a contract is signed, the trial period starts. For a technology product such as an automation system, this includes integrating new hardware and software into existing systems.

- *Many decisions are based on a brand's reputation for onboarding efficiency, so set up processes that will enable you to succeed and exceed expectations for this critical phase of your customers' journey with you.*
- *During the sales process, include detailed information about your technology and ability to integrate easily and quickly, the people leading your implementation processes, schedules you've met, and customer feedback about the ease of setting them up to use your product efficiently and achieve their goals.*

Step 12: Assess satisfaction with product and the brand's responsiveness and service.

❯ Purchasers start assessing the decision they have made in the early stages of installation and use.

- *Check in often during these early stages to assure satisfaction and reassure their decision to choose you to help meet their goals.*
- *Assessing satisfaction early and frequently is key to identifying issues quickly and resolving them before they become a crisis or lead to a lost customer. Satisfaction at every stage of a supplier relationship helps you develop the kind of data and stories you can share with prospects looking for a proven company to help them throughout all stages of a project.*

Step 13: Repeat purchase, assign loyalty, and refer others.

❯ For both simple and complex purchasing decisions, purchasers and consumers will assign loyalty or at least repeat business to brands that successfully address the above steps and deliver on their promises.

- *Leverage customer successes for new sales opportunities by asking happy customers to serve as references for new ones.*
- *Ask for written statements you can share and if they'll be willing to talk to a prospect and answer questions.*
- *This commitment by a current customer adds valuable confidence to prospects going through a lengthy decision process.*
- *Periodically ask customers to consider upgrades or additional products you offer that fill their needs and will help them accelerate their goal fulfillment.*

Step 14: Switch to another brand.

❯ A signed contract is not a sign of a lifetime customer. In fact, customers will willingly lose their deposits or implementation fees paid if things don't go well in the beginning of a relationship. Walking away from a bad choice is costly but many companies would rather lose money upfront over losing more in the long-term from lost productivity and opportunity costs.

- *Hopefully you are not the company that loses customers at implementation. But the fact that this happens presents an opportunity most businesses don't recognize.*
- *If you lose a prospect to another client, and the standard implementation phase for your industry is two to three months, reach out to the lost client in this time period to see how it's going with their supplier of choice. You might be amazed at how many people will tell you they are not happy and open the door to doing business with you again. Having already vetted you out for the prior decision process lessens the time and work involved for them to make a switch.*

The key to successful selling for any business in any industry is to keep the positive energy flowing from introduction to a completed transaction. Creating touch points for each step of the decision journey is a successful way to do this. Regardless of what you sell, and to whom, general consumers or B2B purchasers, decision processes are quite similar in terms of looking for a solution, vetting out product and brand options, selecting brands to try, and assessing satisfaction.

Businesses that sell to other businesses through the process of demos and customized proposals have opportunities to ask questions of prospects, engage in meaningful dialogue to better understand needs and expectations, and then make recommendations for specific needs. For consumer brands, the above is not often the case. If your business is an e-commerce boutique for natural skin care products you make yourself, your first goal is to get a customer to try your product instead of complete a Contact Us form or schedule a product demo. You miss the opportunity to ask what their needs, anticipations, and anxieties may be so that you can customize responses and proposals and spark conversations while prospects compare products, consumer reviews, pricing, and product details. As a result, you need to speak to the decision processes in your product descriptions and pop-ups. For example, if you know a criterion important to your skin care customers is organic ingredients, and you are selling on Amazon along with many others in your category, make this communication clear on your product imagery. Maybe a banner on your product photos stating all organic ingredients. And if price is important to spark a trial with new customers, have a pop-up offering 10 percent off for new customers. If possible, include a link to your live chat service or Frequently Asked Questions page on your website so consumers can learn more before they buy.

Knowing what is important to your targets and communicating those elements while they are reviewing options is key to sparking trial, and without trial there is clearly no repeat business.

Managing the Sales Funnel

Needless to say, all leads don't convert to lifetime customers, let alone a single sale. It's important to track the progress of your leads to assure you are filling your funnel with qualified leads instead of leads with little propensity to convert to revenue. Traditionally, a sales funnel starts when you generate a large number of leads from an event or a campaign, enter them in your lead database or CRM, and then work to nurture them from Leads to Prospects to Proposals and then to Paid Customers. The end goal of funnel management is of course to get the highest number of leads at the top of the funnel down through the layers to the end point which is a closed customer and source of revenue. While this simple process remains the same, the way we manage the various layers of the funnel has changed, and for the better.

CRM tools provide many insights about the contacts in your funnel that enable you to communicate at each stage of their decision journey with precision. These tools also help you see where best to spend your time by scoring leads for you according to which leads have the highest chance to convert, and in some cases, when they are most likely to close.

For example: You attend a trade show and come back with 100 leads that you enter into your CRM database. Upon entry, leads are mostly equal but over time, some will emerge as high priorities and others as low priorities according to response to your marketing campaigns, and/ or their activity with your brand assets. A week after the event, you email all your leads and tell them more information about your products. Some leads will open your email and stop there. Others will open your email, reply via email, and others do what you want them to do—request more information or a sales demo. Your CRM system could be set up to sort the leads according to the above activity and might assign a high lead score to those that replied or clicked an email link to a form asking for a meeting or demo, a moderate score to those that opened but did not click-through to your website or Contact Us form, and a low score to those who did not open at all. Sorting leads by their score helps you see which events you attend that bring you the most interested and qualified leads, and which campaigns you execute that result in the largest number of high-scoring leads. This will help you spend your time and money on activities that have a higher chance of paying off than those that produce low-scoring leads.

Optimizing the Impact of Your CRM System

Many CRM tools on the market now allow you to monitor how leads in your database interact with your brand on social media and your website, what their individual interests are, and record the outcomes of any engage-ment activities such as a sales demo, emails sent, and phone calls. Some tools also let you do some social listening and show you what your leads are posting about on social media, what pages they recently visited on your website and when, and so on.

As you collect leads, make a point to set up contact lists according to where they are in their journeys and your funnel. Then execute relevant and regular email campaigns and automated triggered sequences to keep leads moving in the right direction. The difference between a campaign and a sequence is that a campaign refers to sending the same information to lists of contacts at the same time. A sequence is a series of emails you set up and schedule for automatic delivery to a specified group of leads. If someone responds to an email in the automated sequence, they move out of the sequence into a funnel where they are nurtured one-on-one by a sales rep whose job it is to move them toward a closing pattern.

The key message here is that you need to generate leads via the activities discussed throughout this book and manage these leads with optimized speed, efficiency, and relevance with a CRM system that helps you focus on where leads are according to their decision journey and your sales funnel. Set your CRM system up to give as much information as possible about your leads, which messages/campaigns/actions drive the most engagement, and who on your team is doing the best job of converting. There are numerous CRM systems to choose from that support B2B and B2C businesses. Current considerations include HubSpot, Zoho, Pipe Drive, SalesForce, Monday and Oracle Netsuite. As you are searching look for key functionality across those you are vetting, and then find the one that offers the most value for the features and price.

Key to succeeding with a CRM system is to use it continuously to monitor, score, and reach out to leads. CRMs make it easy to organize prospects, leads, and customers into segments according to their relationships with you and their specific needs and value. Segments for your sales outreach could include:

> Decision journey stage

> Funnel stages

> Source of lead—campaign, sequences, social media, thought leadership, event, etc.

> Lead scores

> Social listening inputs—interests expressed on social media you can address relevantly.

> Cold leads—those never opening an email or taking a call since first introduction.

> Warm leads—those responding in the past 12 months but not engaging or converting.

> Hot leads—those responding to campaigns, engaging in sales calls, and expressing interest

When looking for a CRM tool, keep in mind you can often buy the inexpensive level to start and upgrade as you grow. Be sure to select a program that you can grow with because once you upload your data, input your customer information for your CRM and personalized marketing campaigns, it will be time consuming and pricey to switch.

Partnerships and Resellers

A sales team of one is clearly not going to scale revenue as quickly as a sales team with multiple players. However, growing a sales team is not so easy as it takes time and money to train people to work in your industry and how to hunt and harvest among your target customers. You may not be able to hire people to sell for you as you get out of the starting gates, but you can establish relationships with reseller partners at very little cost to you. Essentially, resellers allow you to exponentially grow your sales force overnight.

There are many types of reselling partners you can consider that differ from relationships you may set up with wholesalers and distributors. Selling partnerships are just that—partnerships with companies that could benefit from referring or selling your products, or from bundling their products with yours for added consumer value. By working with partners, you can expand your sales team, networks, and reach substantially overnight. The key is to find a business that produces or distributes products that are complimentary to yours and work out ways you can add each other's products or services into offerings.

Some examples of selling partnerships include:

Referral Partners: If you are a CPA and looking to add ancillary expertise without adding staff and overhead, it might be a logical fit to partner with a CFP, a certified financial planner, who has clients already inclined to hire out financial services. For every referral they send you that becomes a paying client, you could agree to pay a 20 percent commission and vice versa.

Selling Partners: Beyond referrals, you can align partners that sell your products along with theirs. For example, a producer of floor mats and seat covers for automobiles would want to secure partnerships with automobile dealerships for retail sales. If you offer a service, such as repair for personal or professional equipment, you would want to align partnerships with distributors or sellers of the original goods and ask them to sell service packages that you fulfill.

Affiliate Partners: Affiliate marketing, at the time of this writing, was estimated to be valued at $17 billion worldwide with projections to be closer to $28 billion by 2027. Surprise and yet no surprise about these numbers. For one, affiliate marketing is the new home party business that Mary Kay and Tupperware were for generations past. But instead of inviting your friends to your house for wine and cheese and makeup samples, or to see the coolest thing available for leftovers that are likely to rot in your fridge for weeks, you invite friends to engage with you on on your social media pages and click on hot links to learn more or buy what they see. It's really quite brilliant for people wanting a side hustle for extra income. And it's even more brilliant for brands. Here's how it works.

A consumer with a love of fashion can start a social media page highlighting favorite outfits for nightlife, the office, the public gym, or the sidelines for soccer games. If you see their post on Instagram or Facebook, and see an outfit that you like, you can usually find a hotlink that says something like, *Shop This Look*, or *Shop This Outfit*, which will then take you to an online store from which you can make a purchase. When someone clicks a product link on the page of the social media fashion poster, a little cookie follows them from the social page to the store selling the item. If the shopper completes a transaction within a specified time period, maybe a couple of days or so, that little cookie alerts the store owner to pay the owner of the social media page a commission. Affiliate marketing commissions typically pay the reseller between 3 and 30 percent per transaction.

Authority Hacker compiled some statistics about the role of affiliate marketing in 2023. If you are building a retail business, you really cannot ignore this selling channel for many reasons. It presents an unlimited number of reselling partners that are paid commissions only, adds no overhead and little management costs, and increases brand awareness without any marketing costs. Go figure, right? Some of the impressive stats presented by Authority Hacker for 2023 include:

❯ 16 percent of internet orders in the U.S. were from affiliate marketing.

❯ 81 percent of brands use affiliate marketing to increase brand awareness and drives sales.

❯ 5–25 percent of major brands' online sales are from affiliate marketing.

❯ 20 percent of brand marketers say affiliate marketing is their most successful channel.

Established brands have a jump start in affiliate marketing as their products, and their brand quality, are already known to consumers. However, startup brands can leverage this highly efficient channel as well. Here are some tips for getting started.

Before you can start an affiliate marketing program, you need to set your website up for affiliate sales tracking with tracking software. There are many options for tracking software so spend some time searching to find one that best integrates with your website and budget. Per pricing you can get basic free versions which are just that, basic, or pay around $130 a month for more sophisticated programs.

Once your website is set up for e-commerce and your tracking software is in place, it's time to get started on finding affiliates that can promote your products to their networks and drive sales to your website. You can search social media sites like Instagram, Facebook, YouTube, and X for people that post about products in your category and reach out to spark a conversation, or you can tap an affiliate network, or work with an agency to recruit affiliates for you. Rakuten and Amazon Associates are among some of the top networks.

As you find people that post about your category and have affiliate program links in their posts, pay attention to the number of followers they have and the level of engagement they get with posts for products similar to yours. Needless to say, the more followers your affiliate marketers have the more chances you have of increasing brand awareness and gaining sales through this channel.

Affiliates are often highly tapped influencers in their industries because they produce a lot of content that is relevant or entertaining to audiences. They post often, sometimes daily, and to keep their posts, blogs, videos, and other collateral engaging, they stay on top of consumer trends and interests and have a good pulse on what will garner attention and what will not. Paying attention to the content influencers in your space post, and the engagement they get for specific topics or products, will help you fine tune your own messaging so you can drive more sales via their networks and yours at the same time.

Affiliate marketing works well for B2C retailers and for some B2B categories. Software services tend to sell well through affiliates who are experts in the given technology field, as do other technologies and products that support business operations for small to medium sized businesses. Take the time to research affiliate marketing for your industry and see how it is working for category leaders and competitors. Again, you can choose to set it up yourself or you can hire an agency to set up a comprehensive affiliate program for you.

Leading Customers to Lifetime Value

The process of customer retention has evolved a long way from just keeping customers happy and checking in on them once in a while. It now relies on software programs that let you market to each of your current accounts, and prospects, in highly personalized ways, referencing their specific relationships with your brand, expressed goals, and relevant new opportunities to help you secure each customer's lifetime value (LTV).

As an entrepreneur just getting started, it might not be the right time to invest in a sophisticated and expensive system for account-based marketing but that does not mean you cannot engage in some of the proven practices.

Here are a few tips to help you close marketing leads, and lead them to LTV, a critical outcome for sustainable revenue and growth.

Tip 1: Align your sales process with your ESP strategy.

Emotional selling propositions (ESPs) don't stop with marketing campaigns. Delivering the emotional fulfillment you promise at every step of the journey to lifetime value is critical to keeping people engaged and trusting you with their business and loyalty. If you promise safety and security in your ads, your sales process must deliver on those promises by making customers feel they are working with people that have their interests in mind, can be trusted, and will keep them safe from the problems they seek to avoid.

Tip 2: Tap your customers' decision journey.

Make sure each interaction you have with prospects and leads—email or phone call—aligns with a stepping stone in the customer decision journey. Keep accounts engaged by helping them gain the insights and knowledge they need to make wise decisions. This not only helps improve your open rates for email campaigns, but it will also help get your calls answered and establish you as a partner, not a vendor. This difference alone can make or break a company.

Tip 3: Stay the course.

Persistence wins the game in sales. Yet trends show that most sales executives stop reaching out far too soon. At one point, the rumor was that it took 5–7 touch points via various channels and methods to get a prospect to engage. It's currently a lot more and that is not a trend likely to change. This is why you need to set up automated campaigns to reach out to prospects and customers consistently, make regular phone calls, send personalized messages, and more to keep conversations going and leads moving toward closing patterns.

Once your marketing efforts generate an MQL (marketing qualified lead), which is classified as a prospect responding to a campaign, your sales efforts need to convert that MQL into a SQL, a sales qualified lead. An SQL is a lead that has responded to a sales outreach, e.g., a call, an email, and has expressed interest in moving further down the path to becoming a customer. To keep leads steadfast on the journey to conversion, your outreach needs to be frequent enough to keep your brand top of mind, and meaningful to the decision process. Checklists and other decision support materials are examples of the kind of content that keeps leads interested and moving through your sales pathway.

Tip 4: Ask for the sale.

Seems silly to suggest, but again it's not. Many salespeople do not ask for the sale. It's easy to do a demo, ask for questions at the end, and then sit back and wait for a prospect to call you. Because, hey, who would not want what you have to sell? Not happening. At least not very often. You need to ask prospects giving you their time to learn about your product what they think, what they like, and what they don't like so much. What are they thinking about the timing of their purchase? What are they thinking about you vs. a competitor? Ask if they are interested in seeing a proposal. It's amazing how many sales demos I have watched just to see the salesperson sign off without asking any of these questions. Needless to say, sales were slow to come in. If you don't ask for the next step—a proposal, a purchase, or a next meeting—it likely won't happen period. Asking for the sale applies to working with prospects and current customers who may not think to upgrade or renew if not prompted.

Tip 5: Conduct regular audits.

It goes without saying again that retaining customers is a faster path to profitability and scaling a new company than acquiring new ones as it's far less time consuming and resource draining. However, it's easy to get complacent about the clients you have while you chase after the thrill of a new win. Nothing feels quite like the euphoria we get when we close a hard-won client. It's like watching your favorite team winning the playoffs or the championship title. But chasing new clients and ignoring existing ones is quite often the demise of even the most promising businesses.

You need to continuously conduct customer satisfaction surveys and monitor your NPS score (net promoter score) which tells businesses if customers are likely to refer you to a friend or industry associate. NPS values are a huge indicator of trust and satisfaction as consumers are not going to recommend a brand they don't like or trust as doing so could be embarrassing or damaging to relationships they care about. But sending out an NPS survey once a year is not enough. Go a step further and delve a lot deeper by conducting customer audits which are simply meetings you hold with customers to assess what you are doing right, wrong, and where you can improve.

So, just what does a customer audit look like? At first glance it might look like a long list of survey questions, but when completed it's a very telling story about your business and is often full of big reveals and plot twists.

Audits help you discover realities such as:

Customer satisfaction: Many customers simply won't actively tell you they are not happy. Instead they communicate passively by not renewing their business unexpectedly or cancelling a contract with no warning. An audit can help you avoid this by getting them to tell you how they really feel about your service, product quality, onboarding support, pricing, and a lot more. I've been in the business of marketing for a long time and for as long as that has been, I've interviewed clients' customers to determine satisfaction. Every time I have learned that customers my clients believe are their happiest are not happy and some have been in the process of replacing them altogether. In one case, every customer I called told me they felt the CEO of the company was intentionally misleading about capabilities and so they were looking to make a change. These were the very clients the CEO told me were his best supporters. Clearly a big disconnect which can happen anywhere.

Business Development Performance: Beyond sales closure rates and revenue generated, the best way to determine how effective your sales and business development representatives are at securing and retaining business is to ask your customers. Ask about a rep's professionalism, service ethic, responsiveness, and advisory role. Purchasers across business categories want more than someone who can schedule meetings and process payments. Many want partners that can advise them on strategies and tactics to better reach their goals, not just to give them a good price for a product or service they purchase. If the people you assign to manage your clients are just order takers, plan on losing customers eventually to companies that take orders, provide satisfactory service and quality, and take the time to advise, inform, and inspire clients at the same time.

Opportunities: Talking to clients about their growth plans, profitability goals and operational aspirations can uncover opportunities you might not hear about otherwise. You might discover a client is thinking of hiring a videographer to produce short videos for social media posts when you also provide that competency. Discovering this need, and their apparent lack of awareness of your skillset to meet this need, opens up conversations that can lead to increased revenue for you and optimized efficiency for them. You might discover something you are doing is paying off more than you knew, which gives you some leverage for extending contracts or adding to your scope of work.

Customer audits are primarily about listening to customers to learn what you are doing right, what you are doing wrong, new challenges they face, growth plans for their company that you can help realize, and so on. They are also a great opportunity to present new capabilities and related achievements of you and your team. As you take notes and listen to needs of your clients, be prepared to present anecdotal case studies about related achievements for similar clients and new capabilities you've developed since they first signed with you. This furthers the powerful outcomes of social proof and authority we've discussed earlier.

The underlying success for all customer audits is simply this: Listen and come back with a plan for how you can help them do more with less, achieve more of their goals with your products or services, and what you can do for their bottom line in the next 6–12 months. Don't wait to be asked. Customer audits are a big carpe diem opportunity you simply cannot skip. My friend Mary Noyes, an entrepreneur who helped set up several organizations attributes her success to a single word—"listening." Per Mary, "listening is an art form and a powerful catalyst for collaboration and evolution." Beyond listening, she is considerate. She takes the time to hear what a client needs to achieve their goals learning more about their persona, not just the revenue line. By being authentic and attentive in her relationships, they build trust with her.

Tip 6: Build a Decision Support Journey

Decision processes for complex and simple purchases are becoming more complex as the options are greater than before for customers, and so too is the criteria many purchasers expect brands to meet. Inserting yourself randomly in a decision journey without a well concerted plan is like throwing spaghetti at the wall. It doesn't look good and results don't stick for long. Take the time to map out a decision process journey and assign actions you can execute at each step. Here's an example of what that could look like:

	Customer Decision Process	Decision Support
Introduction	Meet Potential Providers	Show empathy toward goals and experience fulfilling
Step 1	Vet Providers for Relevance	Present case studies to show success for similar customers
Step 2	Sales Demo, Initial Call/Meeting	Share testimonials, relevant work examples
Step 3	Proposal Requested	Submit proposal with distinctions that set brand apart
Step 4	Brand Reputation Reviews	Share links to social media, thought leaderships posts, testimonials
Step 5	Onsite Meetings	Introduce SMEs at all levels of company
Step 6	Meet to Discuss Vetting Notes	Send industry news to showcase brand intelligence/awareness
Step 7	Ponder Decision	Send decision support guides that are objective

When you can build content and touch points for every step of a customer journey, you have a much higher chance of your marketing and selling actions paying off. You are no longer just a brand making promises in hopes of getting the win. You become a partner sharing valuable information to help others make wise and informed choices.

GO TIME

There are many critical steps outlined in this chapter you need to map out in your marketing plan. Here's a summary:

Step 1: Map out the decision process for purchasers in your business category when choosing products and brands. Don't assume you know this path well. Ask leaders in your category, read research reports, and ask your customers about the criteria used to select you, and why they chose you over other options, and why they stay with you.

Step 2: Identify the needs that decision processes are set up to fill. Document these elements from the customers' perspective and then outline your ability to deliver on expectations for each solution or need sought.

Step 3: Select a CRM tool that will help you manage your sales funnel and monitor the impact your sales approach and team are having on moving each account to conversion.

Step 4: Set up your customer retention processes. The first step here is to build a list of questions you need to cover when you meet with your customers for a bi-annual audit. Next step is to reach out to your customers and set up live, in-person meetings. Making the effort to meet in person instead of on a virtual meeting channel can have a much bigger impact than you think. If a customer matters to you, show it in actions, incentives, rewards, customized pricing and the like, not just words.

Step 5: Map out the Decision Support Journey that aligns with customers decision processes. This will help you connect at the right time with the right communications, content, and incentives for each step of the decision process for your customers.

In short, the key to successful selling is to find a way to balance your customer acquisition needs with your customer retention mandates. That old adage about it costing a lot more to gain new clients than it does to retain old ones is not old school thinking. It is actually becoming more relevant all the time. Just expect the cost of acquisition to get higher as we remain in markets where customers have more options, trust less, and have easier pathways for switching brands.

CHAPTER 12

Pulling It All Together

It's easy to feel overwhelmed when you finish a book about all the many and wonderful things you need to do to succeed. Daunting maybe, but only if you let it be. This chapter shares perspectives about marketing in general, how to keep it real, how to keep your brand real, and tips for making it fun and rewarding.

You'll read about:

> The power of authenticity in all you do

> The reveal about marketing in today's fast changing culture and marketplace

> Tips for making marketing as manageable as getting out of bed every day

We've covered a lot of topics and tactics in this book. All of which are doable if you are truly committed to building a sustainable business. The principles and actions outlined in this book can and will help you grow your business if you stay true to a marketing routine. We have talked about values throughout this book such as of CSR, ESG, and virtues associated with integrity and transparency. One of the most powerful brand attributes you can develop through your marketing is authenticity, one of the new power metrics for brands.

A research boutique in Los Angeles, California, Breakthrough Research, studies the impact of authenticity on brands and releases an annual Brand Authenticity report. For 2023, 5,000 respondents reviewed 100 national brands doing business in the U.S. and scored them for authenticity in what they say, do, and deliver. The top drivers for brands deemed as authentic by respondents were a brand's perceived integrity, ability to connect with consumers, and offering accessible prices. Attributes for which respondents scored the 100 brands presented to them included being ethical, wholesome, offering high quality products and services, relatability, and fair pricing. Attributes that we tend to think matter that actually scored low in this 2023 report included being fun, creative, traditional, having a rich history, helping people express themselves, and being adventurous or trendy.

Leading with Authenticity

In addition to attributes that create a sense of authenticity, actions that up authenticity scores for businesses include treating customers well, owning up to mistakes, and caring about the social impact of their business, e.g., CSR and ESG activities. Outcomes associated with brand authenticity include positive first impressions, longer lasting connections with brands, better performance on the stock market, and better perceived product quality.

Influencers and affiliate marketers mentioned in Chapter 11 highlight the importance of authenticity in a world that is ripe with misinformation, and way too many fake promises and schemes. To build a large network of followers and keep them engaged with social media posts to the point they click on shopping links and make purchases from affiliate brands, influencers need to be real, raw, and completely authentic. Being authentic means exposing your human side, ups and downs, not just an image of perfection which has often been the norm in business for many years. It also means showing your customers and prospects that you are just like them in many ways. Across all industries, we trust business representatives we can relate to as they are "just like us" more than those we cannot relate to as they seem too different to be part of our trusted tribe. We also follow people like us, or people who project who we want to be, on social media. We want to see how people in similar situations overcame challenges or capitalized on opportunities. And we are influenced by those people daring to be authentically themselves without embarrassment or hesitation. A friend of mine's success as a blogger and influencer for middle-aged women embodies the power of authenticity. Here's a bit of the backstory.

Nanette Johnson's life was changing. Her kids were growing up and leaving home, leaving her with not just an empty nest, but a changing identity. Like many parents, her life stories for many years largely focused on her kids' activities, and their identities. As she and her friends in the same phase of life turned the page into a new chapter, she quickly discovered that this was not so easy for everyone. So, she started writing. She started a blog and wrote about the upside of life's ever winding journey, sharing her own ups and downs, fears and anticipations, exposing her real side and giving others comfort and confidence to do the same. Some of her breakout posts included stories of anxiety about traveling on airplanes (who can't relate to that), and breaking her diet soda habit (again, who can't somewhat relate to that). She shows her vulnerabilities and exposes her real and raw self. She also discovered wearing fun clothes that made her feel powerful and energetic was key to making her own life's passage more enjoyable. To her, fashion had a way of making her feel connected to the bigger world outside of mothering and working a full-time job. So, Nanette turned her blog, SweetFringeBenefits, into a fashion affiliate marketing business using Instagram as her primary channel. Her posts and reels tell stories about moments in her life that her followers can relate to and showcase her contagious enthusiasm for helping others find their best self. As you watch her sparkle showing off a new style that helps her project her best self, you want to be part of it! You want the same enthusiasm and confidence you see in a person you believe is real, just like you.

The "real" side about Nanette that creates so much attention and online love for her is that she is not 5.11 and 105 pounds. She is 5.3 and vacillates between large and extra-large in most of the clothing she features, and very openly reveals the sizes she wears. Being real has helped her build a very real following of thousands of Instagram and Facebook users who want to be a little bit like her. In just two years, she went from a storyteller to an influencer brands want to align with. Brands now seek her out and ask her to feature their products in her posts, and her revenue just continues to grow.

I share this story because her example presents a very important lesson for marketers in all categories, across all industries. Be authentic. Be yourself. And dare to share. Share your truths, share your vulnerabilities and successes, share your intent to improve the lives of others, and share your commitment to ethics for how you treat customers, source your products, and operate your business.

Some tips we learn from successful influencers include:

▶ Create stories that followers can relate to on emotional and functional levels.

▶ Post content often to build followers and connect with algorithms that align with search engines for Google and social media platforms.

▶ Use multiple channels to broaden your reach.

▶ Show your brand's authenticity by showcasing the humanness of you and your team.

▶ Invite others to comment on your stories and tell theirs alongside yours. The more comments, likes, and shares you get, the more your pages show up in searches.

When you can share your stories as an entrepreneur, those about your challenges and successes, you become real, and really attractive to people whose stories are like yours but might feel they are alone in their struggles to reach their goals.

The Reality about Marketing

No surprise likely here, but one of the greatest obstacles to achieving marketing success is you. By reading this book, you now have a solid understanding of the programs you need to develop, the actions you need to take, and the strategies you need to execute. Many entrepreneurs start off with a great enthusiasm to do most if not all of the actions discussed throughout this book. But as the days get long and the to-do lists get even longer, marketing activities often get pushed down the list of priorities and become "someday" projects. When this happens, brands struggle to break out and thrive, especially if competitors have well oiled marketing machines that keep building awareness, followers, and customers. Just know, even if you are a business of one, you can establish efficient processes and find the support you need to execute a sustainable marketing program for launching your business and growing it to where you want it to be.

Finding Affordable Resources

Resources you can access by the project and use only as you need them vs. include in your payroll and overhead include:

❭ Freelance website developers for your DIY website

❭ Copy writers or ChatGPT editors

❭ Social media managers—build your pages, post for you, respond with your messaging and nurture leads to engage with your brand.

❭ Website developers and managers—design and maintain your site's pages and content.

❭ Graphic designers—create your print and digital display ads, banner ads, update elements for your website and other brand assets, create templates for reports, brochures print materials, and more.

You can find freelancers for all of the above and more by browsing LinkedIn or via companies that match freelancers for a wide range of marketing support skills with businesses like yours. As of this writing, some of the top sites for finding freelancers are Fiverr, Upwork, and Toptal. But browse a lot of the results when you google "marketing freelancers" to compare talent, reviews, prices, and terms and conditions.

Just like it takes multiple touch points to get a lead to engage with you, marketing takes time. Time for you to set up a well-thought-out plan based upon market and consumer insights, and time devoted to execution every week, and sometimes every day. And it does not stop when you reach your revenue goals. Marketing is a constant.

Keeping It Real and Keeping It Fun

No offense to the accountants, investors, engineers, and operations managers of the world, but marketing is truly the most fun aspect of business. We not only get to use our business skills, we get to imagine. It is on us to come up with fun ideas that connect our brands to communities and people. Marketing spins on imagination and innovation, and the more you imagine for your customer experiences, and innovate communications strategies that tap the psychology of choice and spark loyalty, the more fun you will have growing toward your goals.

Back to the company I highlighted in Chapter 1 on value and purpose, Cotopaxi. When founder Davis Smith launched his new company, he knew he only had one chance to make good first impressions for a new brand in an old and very cluttered industry, adventure apparel. Buying media across social and advertising channels is expensive for startups so Davis imagined a fun way he could get others to post about his products and company on their social channels, introducing thousands of people outside his own networks to his new brand. The innovative Go-to-Market event he pulled off was not just successful for getting a new brand launched, it became a popular annual event.

Davis and his team crafted what he called a Questival, a celebration of people adventuring and doing good together. They organized a 24-hour team adventure race that required participants to do adventurous and service-based activities to earn points and promoted this event on college campuses.

Participating teams received Cotopaxi backpacks to use during their adventure and earned points by completing the list of challenges presented to them, doing outdoor activities or community service together and posting stories about their adventures which showed off the brand's products and values. A Questival challenge or activity may be eating as many pickles as you can in 15 seconds, cleaning up a local park, sparking a fitness challenge in public among strangers, and completing a service project or random act of kindness. Teams completing the challenges were scored and the top achievers won prizes including Cotopaxi gear.

The first year drew 5,000 Questival participants and more than 30,000 social posts reaching networks of thousands of people beyond those participating. Questival was quickly made a yearly event, taking place in multiple locations to share the adventures, impact of service, and of course brand identity. This event is a great example of how imagining and then executing can create memorable customer experiences, spark awareness, and create loyal enthusiasts for your brand.

Marketing has changed dramatically since the days of the 4 Ps: product, place, promotion, and price. It is the catalyst to the greatest contributor of success for any business in any field: meaningful relationships with audience groups that provide fulfillment beyond just the function of the product sold or the satisfaction of the service rendered. As an entrepreneur, you have more technology than ever before to help you identify your most qualified prospects and customers and nurture them to lifetime value. And as discussed throughout this book, so much marketing technology allows you to set up automated campaigns, which means you will still have time to run your business while you generate and convert leads.

So now what? There's one last step toward marketing success. The most critical one of all.

Get started!

About the Author

A marketing junkie since graduating college with a journalism degree, Jeanette McMurtry led Fortune 500 companies and startups to marketing success through her approach to Psychology Based Marketing. Instead of crafting campaigns around worn-out business concepts like Unique Selling Propositions and VIP loyalty programs, she has helped brands across industries develop and appeal to ESPs (emotional selling propositions), which tap the unconscious mind and appeal to the psychology of choice.

Jeanette is the author of four marketing books starting with *Big Business Marketing for Small Business Budgets* (McGraw-Hill), *Marketing for Dummies 5th Edition* (Wiley), *Marketing for Dummies 6th Edition* (Wiley), *and Market Your Business: Your Do It Yourself Guide to Marketing* (Entrepreneur). Beyond serving in executive positions and as a consultant in various industries, her career includes keynote presentations around the globe, marketing workshops for brands and associations, monthly columns for global media, and helping brands in multiple industries achieve marketing and sales success. Jeanette has also served as a Chief Marketing Officer for financial services, software/SaaS, and higher education organizations.

When not crafting marketing campaigns, writing, or losing herself in historical fiction, Jeanette enjoys gaining inspiration and solace from her inspiring family, which includes three powerful and hard to keep up with daughters and many beloved canine and feline children, as well as long walks in Colorado's high country or around the lighthouses in Maine's mystic waterfront villages.

Acknowledgements

A huge thank you to my family and friends for their undying and very appreciated support throughout this journey. My immediate tribe, John, Jessica, Jenevieve, Jordan, and dear friends who redefine friendship, John and Chris Hostetter. Thank you to Mary Noyes and David Hasson for sharing their world and beautiful home on the sea in Maine with me, a most inspiring place to write.

Index